Twayne's United States Authors Series

Sylvia E. Bowman, *Editor*

INDIANA UNIVERSITY

Glenway Wescott

GLENWAY WESCOTT

GLENWAY WESCOTT

by WILLIAM H. RUECKERT

University of Rochester

 87

Twayne Publishers, Inc.   ::   New York

Library of Congress Catalog Card Number: 65-18906

MANUFACTURED IN THE UNITED STATES OF AMERICA BY
UNITED PRINTING SERVICES, INC.
NEW HAVEN, CONN.

FOR
BETTY
WHO WORRIED OVER IT

GLENWAY WESCOTT

by

WILLIAM H. RUECKERT

This first book-length appraisal of Glenway Wescott recognizes him as one of the more interesting and important writers of our time. Author of *The Pilgrim Hawk*, a work that has become a model of the short novel form, Wescott has been for too long relegated to the secure but not very exciting position of a man of letters who happens to have written one minor masterpiece. The aim of this study is to discuss chronologically nearly fifty years—from 1920 to the present—in the development of a writer in immediate touch with the significant events and departures of his time.

Each of Glenway Wescott's works is considered separately, but its overall place in the body of his output is never lost sight of. His role as a man of letters is seen as organic to such titles as *The Pilgrim Hawk* and his brilliant longer novel, *The Grandmothers*.

The continuing vitality of Glenway Wescott's career—and the paradox of a writer involved with and unjustly overshadowed by some of his more flamboyant contemporaries and friends—is emphasized in a final chapter, where his lasting achievement as an artist is keenly appreciated and placed in its proper focus.

For a complete listing of titles in TWAYNE'S UNITED STATES AUTHORS, ENGLISH AUTHORS, and UNITED STATES CLASSICS SERIES please see reverse side of this jacket.

Preface

TO WRITE of a living author is to contemplate the strange complexities of organic growth and to set oneself the task of fixing the form of a man's works while it is still in the process of shaping. In the spring of 1945 one would have said, almost positively, that Glenway Wescott had inexplicably completed his growth at the age of forty-four with *Apartment in Athens* and that the essays published since then were only sporadic attempts which in no way changed the essential shape of his total body of work. But in the summer of 1962 there came an announcement that a new book—*Images of Truth*—was to appear in the fall and that an omnibus collection—*A Windfall*—was to appear in the spring of 1963.

To anyone familiar with Wescott's work, this news was an indication that a new period of growth had apparently begun, for his career as a writer has been characterized by spurts of books which have come out of intensely creative periods of varying lengths. Only in the beginning (from 1920 to 1927) was he regularly productive: five books, counting the poetry, in eight years; from then on, he published in fits and starts. A short burst in 1930 produced *The Babe's Bed;* a longer one in 1932-33 produced *Fear and Trembling* and *A Calendar of Saints for Unbelievers;* an even longer and extraordinarily productive one from 1939 to 1944 brought forth one first-rate work after another in a great variety of forms (poetry, ballet libretto, essay, and fiction) and seemed to indicate that, at last, Wescott had realized his great talent; then, for seventeen years, widely separated fits and starts produced, with the single exception of *Twelve Fables of Aesop* in 1954, only reviews and essays.

The new book—*Images of Truth: Remembrances and Criticism* —is a coherent collection of eight critical-personal, sometimes autobiographical, essays about fiction. As is true of most of Wescott's work (the main exception is *Apartment in Athens*) the mode is essentially lyric; the coherence comes not so much from the subject matter as from Wescott's experience of the author and his work. The real center of the book is not fiction but Wescott, and the power of the book is dependent upon the quality of Wescott's experience and upon the form and style he has developed to express it. Neither the lyric mode nor the lyric essay is new to Wescott: he began as a lyric poet, wrote fiction that is best understood as being essentially lyric, and as early as 1930 wrote a lyric essay about Elizabeth Madox Roberts. In some ways, then, *Images of Truth* is not new growth at all; for the lyric mode, though he has frequently denied it, has always been the true creative center from which all of Wescott's best work has come, and the lyric essay has long been one of the characteristic forms in which he has done some of his best work. But the work is new in at least two important ways: it apparently completes a development that has an almost classical symmetry and at the same time develops a form that seems to be as native to America as it is organic for Wescott.

Wescott's work is peculiar for two main reasons: he was a potentially major writer who lapsed into minority, and his work does not really become significant until it is viewed as a whole and in terms of his development right up to the present. Some of his essays (the ones on Fitzgerald and Porter, for example) can stand alone, but even his one authentic master work, *The Pilgrim Hawk*, is most profitably viewed in context: as a fictional sequel to *The Grandmothers*; as a bringing to perfection of the form first used in *The Babe's Bed*; as the fictional counterpart to the essay "Good-Bye Wisconsin," in which, fictionally disguised again as Alwyn Tower, he says good-bye to prose-fiction; and as a perpetual sad reminder of what, with retrospective irony, one feels Wescott might have done had he been able or willing to follow the true creative direction of his talent. *Apartment in Athens*, which might stand alone as a didactic war novel—a piece of fictional propaganda—is also best understood in a developmental context: as the translation into European and political terms of the old American and Puritan dilemma dealt with in *The Grandmothers*; as the second (*Fear and Trembling* was the first) and last deliberately polemical, public-spirited work; as the last published experiment in prose-fiction; and as a work of prose-fiction which, unlike all of his others, derives not from his true creative center but from some abstract idea Wescott has had since 1930 of what prose-fiction ought to be.

Wescott's involuting development must now include *Images of Truth*, and that book changes the shape of his works because it adds a significant stage to his development as a writer. Instead of writing prose-fiction, he now writes prose about fiction and his inability to write it—but in a form that often so closely resembles that of his best fictional work (*The Grandmothers, The Babe's Bed, The Pilgrim Hawk,* "The Dream of Audubon") that one does not know sometimes, as one did not always know with the above works, whether to call it prose or fiction. The happiest solution, as with the best work of E. B. White, is to invent new terms which more accurately describe the essential characteristics of these mixed forms. Like the novels, the essays are lyric, but the disguised "I" of the novels, usually Alwyn Tower, has become Wescott, speaking in the same mode and with the same tendencies—toward abstraction and symbolic loading—but now in his own voice. The essays represent a direct approach to the truth of the title, but Wescott has dispensed with the making of images, fictional or poetic; he has given up the fictional disguises, which he seems to have experienced as violations of his own integrity, and has gone directly through his own self, with his own kind of sometimes embarrassing honesty, to the images of others, and through them to multiple truths about himself, his experience, the artist, his work, the world, and assorted timeless verities.

The new stage, then, is at least five-fold: the direct approach; the total commitment to truth-saying but in a non-polemical way; the open approach to truth through the self; the apparently final switch from prose-fiction to prose about fiction; and the bringing to perfection of the lyric essay. The new stage, like all stages in Wescott's development, and perhaps like any stage after the first in anyone's development, is new growth from old, with all the repetition and variation one always finds in such growth. In this sense, it is part (and for purposes of this study, the last part) of a long, slow organic development which began with eighteen short lyric poems in 1920. Like his life—which can be characterized by Wescott's departure from and return to his mother, his family, and the family enclave—his career as a writer is characterized by departure, innovation, exploration, and return to the point of departure. Wescott's development, though long and in its own way extensive, has really been quite narrow and is finally, like his work, limited. But it has the perfection of its narrowness and limitations and, I think, a valuable beauty.

There is nothing big in Wescott save perhaps *Fear and Trembling,* and that book was mostly a big and bitter failure, pulped by Harpers after only seven hundred and fifty copies had been sold. Yet Wescott has played most of the literary tunes of America since 1920, and in so doing has created a small, almost immaculately symmetrical body of works which are both the verbal counterpart of his own integrity and a record in miniature of many of the significant literary developments in this country during the last thirty years. Like so many minor writers, he is a partial index to his own place and time and may be approached as one section in a larger chapter of cultural history. But it would be an injustice to treat him only in this way, for some of his works have an intrinsic value that transcends cultural or literary history, his development as a writer has a unity and a meaning which make it worth studying for its own sake, and certain readily observable connections between his life and works provide one with an ideal body of material in which to study some of the complex interrelations between the self, society, and literature.

In this study I have attempted to treat all of the above main points more or less simultaneously. In order to do this I have organized the book in terms of two time sequences: the chronological order in which Wescott's books and other writings were published, and the development of Wescott as a writer. I have treated Wescott's development as inherent in the works (rather than the life) and have at all times concentrated on the character of these works and on Wescott the writer rather than on Wescott the man. The order in which I take up the works—since this book aims at thoroughness, I have tried to discuss everything—has been determined almost entirely and somewhat mechanically by the date of publication. Into this double framework of external fact and internal development I have introduced the other significant points as they became relevant and either dispensed with them at once or carried them forward with the chronology and development until I had nothing more to say about them.

Of the ten chapters, nine are organized according to this double framework and attempt to chart and evaluate Wescott's development and achievement up to the present. Since he is still living and productive, and since many things point now, as they did in the 1920's, toward an as yet unachieved greatness, one must be tentative in one's conclusions. The tenth chapter, which is an attempt at placement and general assessment, is therefore only partly conclusive; though many—perhaps most— of the returns are in, Wescott's career indicates that he is certainly capable of a final stage which would make a reassessment necessary. No one but Wescott knows what he has stored in his memory or whether all these years since *Apartment in Athens* have been a long, slow gestation from which will come other masterworks comparable to or better than *The Pilgrim Hawk.* My own conclusion, and a major theme of this book, is that Wescott's career up to the present has been that of an unfulfilled (not wasted) talent. Because I have been waiting many years now for the hawk to fly again (which is probably why there is a slightly melancholy tone throughout), I hope that all of the last chapter proves to have been tentative and that when someone comes to write a later book on Wescott it will have another theme.

Though I have never met him or even corresponded with him, I would like to thank Sy M. Kahn, whose earlier labors made my own so much lighter. The students in the senior honors seminars at the University of Illinois, in which I frequently taught *The Grandmothers* and *The Pilgrim Hawk,* contributed immeasurably to my own understanding of these two works. I would like publicly to thank them. I would also like to thank the following for making available to me Wescott material which I needed: Kerker Quinn; the University of Illinois Library, which bought or borrowed whatever I needed whenever I asked; the Northwestern University Library; the University of Texas Library; and the Library of Congress. I am once again indebted to the Research Board of the University of Illinois for financing two complete typings of the manuscript. And, finally, I am grateful to Glenway Wescott who, in addition to sending me the material listed in the Bibliography, Part I, Unpublished material, kindly sent me the uncorrected galleys of *Images of Truth* so that I might read that book before starting this one, and who patiently answered my inquiries at a time when he was extremely busy with literary labors of his own.

WILLIAM H. RUECKERT

University of Illinois

Acknowledgments

Thanks are due the following persons and organizations for permission to reprint quotations from copyrighted materials. To Harper & Row, Publishers, Inc., for *The Apple of the Eye,* The Dial Press, 1924, Copyright, 1924 by Dial Press, Incorporated; *The Grandmothers,* Harper's Modern Classics Edition, Harper & Brothers, 1927, 1950, Copyright 1927, 1950 by Harper & Brothers, Inc.; *Good-Bye Wisconsin,* Harper & Brothers, 1928, Copyright, 1928, by Harper & Brothers, Copyright renewed 1955, by Glenway Wescott; *Fear and Trembling,* Harper & Brothers, 1932. Copyright, 1932, by Glenway Wescott; *A Calendar of Saints for Unbelievers,* Harper & Brothers, 1933, Copyright 1933, by Glenway Wescott; *The Pilgrim Hawk,* Harper & Brothers, 1940, Copyright 1940, by Harper & Brothers; *Images of Truth,* Harper & Row, 1962, Copyright 1939, 1947, 1951, 1960, 1962 by Glenway Wescott. To Appleton-Century-Crofts for Joseph Warren Beach, *The Twentieth Century Novel: Studies in Technique,* D. Appleton-Century Company, Inc., 1932, Copyright 1932, by The Century Co. To The Viking Press for Frederick J. Hoffman, *The Twenties,* The Viking Press, 1955, Copyright 1949, 1953, 1955, by Frederick J. Hoffman. To the National Council of Teachers of English for C. E. Schorer's "The Maturing of Glenway Wescott," in Vol. XVIII of *College English,* Copyright 1957, by National Council of Teachers of English. To Glenway Wescott for *The Bitterns,* Monroe Wheeler, 1920, Copyright 1920, by Monroe Wheeler; *Natives of Rock,* Francesco Bianco, 1925, Copyright 1926, by Francesco Bianco; *The Babe's Bed,* Harrison of Paris, 1930, Copyright 1930, by Glenway Wescott; "The Dream of Audubon," *The Best One-Act Plays of 1940,* Dodd, Mead & Company, 1941, Copyright 1941, by Dodd, Mead and Company, Inc.

Contents

Chronology

1901   Glenway Wescott born in Kewaskum, Wisconsin—the first of six children.

1914   Leaves home because of difficulties with his father and lives with his uncle and others while attending high school.

1917   Graduates from high school and enters the University of Chicago in the fall. He joins a very lively Poetry Club during his first year and begins writing poetry.

1918   Wescott has never married, but he was engaged from 1918 to 1921. Though it is not clear how much of the story "Bad Han" he actually writes at this time, he begins it.

1919   This is Wescott's early dark year. He has a prolonged illness, attempts suicide, and, because of poor health, withdraws from the University of Chicago after a year and a half. His formal education ends at this point. He works briefly in Chicago and then goes to New Mexico, where he stays with Yvor Winters. By his own account, the time spent in New Mexico is one of the happiest periods of his life.

1920   He returns to Wisconsin to visit his family and then goes to Chicago, where he stays with Monroe Wheeler. *The Bitterns* is published.

1921   Wescott's thirteen years of restlessness and travel begin when he goes first to the Berkshires with Monroe Wheeler for the summer, thence to New York City, and finally to England and Germany (still with Monroe Wheeler), where he stays for nearly a year. Though he is still writing poetry, he begins serious work on "Bad Han" in the Berkshires.

1922   He returns to New York City, where he shares an apartment with Monroe Wheeler and then makes a second trip to Europe, this time as a private secretary.

1923   He returns to New York and again stays with Monroe Wheeler. During this period Wescott writes most of his reviews for *The Dial* and *The New Republic*, and is actively involved with many of the little magazines.

1924 *The Apple of the Eye* is published.

1925 Wescott begins his eight years of expatriation by moving to France. *Natives of Rock* is published.

1926 Wescott begins the pattern of return visits to his family which is to last until 1929. He returns for brief visits in 1926, 1927, 1928, and 1929.

1927 *The Grandmothers* is published. It is a Harper's Prize novel and is a great public and critical success.

1928 *Good-Bye Wisconsin* is published. Wescott is regarded as something of a prodigy of American letters.

1930 *The Babe's Bed* is written and published after one of Wescott's last return trips to visit his family.

1931 With Monroe Wheeler, Barbara Harrison, and George P. Lynes, Wescott takes the German trip which was to result in his writing *Fear and Trembling*.

1932 *Fear and Trembling* and *A Calendar of Saints for Unbelievers* are published and are immediate failures.

1933 Wescott decides that Europe has become a "rat trap" for him and ends his expatriation. After his return he lives both in New York City, where he shares an apartment with his brother, Monroe Wheeler, and George P. Lynes, and in rural New Jersey, where his family has settled after leaving Wisconsin.

1935 Wescott's brother marries Barbara Harrison and Wescott accompanies them to Europe.

1938 Makes another trip to Europe for what he calls "inspirational" reasons.

1939 By his own account, this is when he decides that he finally feels at home here in America. He also begins publishing again after the dry years between 1933 and 1939.

1940 One fine work after another begins to come from his hand: these include "The Dream of Audubon," *The Pilgrim Hawk*, "Summer Ending," and the essay-review on Katherine Anne Porter.

1943 Moves permanently to rural New Jersey.

1945 *Apartment in Athens,* Wescott's last novel, is published, bringing this second period of productivity to an end.

1947 Wescott is elected to the National Institute of Arts and Letters and begins a period of public service to arts and letters which has continued to the present.

1948 Member of the National Commission for UNESCO.

1952 Wescott makes another trip to Europe.

1953 Wescott's father dies. The difficulties between them, Wescott says, have long ago been settled.

1954 *Twelve Fables of Aesop* is published.

1958 Wescott is elected president of the National Institute of Arts and Letters and serves in this capacity until 1961.

1960 Wescott's mother dies. His devotion to her has been life-long and her influence upon him profound.

1962 *Images of Truth* is published. Wescott makes a long and very successful lecture tour which takes him all over the country.

1963 Receives an honorary Doctor of Literature from Rutgers University.

Glenway Wescott

CHAPTER 1

Images and Truth, 1920–1925

I

G LENWAY WESCOTT'S public career as a writer begins
with *The Bitterns*, a small book of lyric poems published
privately in 1920 by his life-long friend Monroe Wheeler and
dedicated to his friend and fellow poet, Arthur Yvor Winters.
The Bitterns contains eleven short poems (the longest is twenty
lines) and one longer poem made up of seven short lyrics. The
prevailing tone—the recurrent lyric stance—is established in the
title poem, which makes explicit the pun in the title. Technically,
the poems range from perfectly formal to perfectly "free," with
the majority tending toward irregularity of meter and loose or
arbitrary rhyme schemes. The tendency of the collection as a
whole is clearly toward free Imagistic poems and, with two or
three exceptions, toward a cold, decorous formality.

In 1925, Wescott had another book of poems published, this
time by Francesco Bianco in a very elegant limited edition
which included ornate black and white floral "decorations" by
Pamela Bianco. There are twenty poems in *Natives of Rock*, all
short, unrhymed, irregular lyrics in the Imagist manner. Again,
the title poem sets the tone for the book as a whole; it describes
a region where "the fire cut away/the soft forest/down to the
rose-pink rock/harder than light," and this could well describe
the poems, most of which are natives of this "rose-pink rock"
and "harder than light" (2). Although published five years after
The Bitterns, the poems in *Natives of Rock*, as the subtitle
XX Poems: 1921-1922 indicates, belong to the same early period
and are best understood as the completion or perfection of the
Imagist form which emerges as the dominant one in *The
Bitterns*. Characteristically, once he has perfected a form, he

seldom uses it again. He never published another book of poems; and, though he may have written a great many, he published only a few more in the 1920's and one more—"Summer Ending"—since then.

After 1922, Wescott was finished with poetry and was ready to move on to something new. During this same period and through 1925, Wescott also wrote book reviews for *Poetry, The New Republic,* and *The Dial.* Like his poetry, the reviews are the elegant work of a precocious young man: each one is meticulously written in a clean, precise, and often witty style. The wit, often barbed, is very unusual in Wescott's work (though not, apparently, in his life); and these reviews, though often excellent, are really atypical in the sense that they represent a form of verbal expression which Wescott publicly pursued only one other time, in *A Calendar of Saints for Unbelievers* (1932), itself an atypical work which represents the nadir of Wescott's achievement in the 1930's and is a clear deflection from the true creative sources of his being. As so many of the books on the 1920's point out, Wescott, a kind of golden boy from the Midwest, was also directly involved in a minor way with the life (and death) of many of the little magazines and, generally, in the cultural and artistic life of the period. This interest, though not always the direct involvement, has persisted to the present time. During the dry periods, when he was unable to be a worker in the arts, Wescott has always been a worker for them, whether in public, as with the National Institute of Arts and Letters, or in private.

In the summer of 1921, while he was still writing poetry and book reviews, Wescott began (or resumed, since he says he started "Bad Han" in 1918) serious work on the long story which was to be his first published prose-fiction (in *The Dial,* 1924) and was to signal the beginning of his often interrupted career as a narrator. Like the poems and book reviews, the story is an example of Wescott's search for the proper medium: but, unlike the poems and reviews, it represents an early experiment in a form which Wescott did not publicly relinquish until 1945 and, perhaps, since he is still vigorous and productive, has not yet completely relinquished. The story is unlike the poems and reviews in two other important ways: it is the first serious use Wescott makes of the so-called regional or Wisconsin material—

the majority of the poems come out of the Chicago, New Mexico, Berkshires, or German experiences—and it announces and treats many of the themes which have concerned him ever since. This same summer Wescott began the eastward movement and subsequent return westward that is almost inescapably symbolic in the lives and imaginations of American writers. Between 1921 and 1924 Wescott made two such journeys eastward. He moved initially from Chicago to Massachusetts to New York City to England to the Continent and finally back to New York City. And then, having first given up Wisconsin and subsequently the Midwest as places in which to live and grow (though not as a source of material, for he lived—or relived—most of his imaginative life there until 1930), he made a second journey from New York City to Europe and back to New York City in 1922-23.[1]

In 1924, Wescott's first novel, *The Apple of the Eye*, was published, and in 1925 he began his eight-year period of expatriation, most of which was spent in France. These two events mark the end of Wescott's beginnings as a writer, a period in which his geographical movements are the physical parallels to his experiments in a variety of art forms. It was a period of "random castings," of trying many things in response to an urgent need to live in accordance with the promptings of the self and to create, in some form, in order to satisfy the impulse toward art which emerged very early in Wescott and was always very powerful and of great purity. By the end of this period he had settled on the form—prose fiction—and in a new place; these two decisions enabled him to achieve some kind of balance and to begin a rich, productive period which lasted until 1933 when he returned to America for good.

II

At best, Wescott's achievements as a poet are minor,[2] as is his place in the history of poetry in the early 1920's. His first book of poetry, for example, has no cultural or historical importance whatsoever and is interesting primarily for organic and personal reasons. *The Bitterns* is most justly assessed as juvenilia, for most of the poems belong to the anonymous lyric outcries of youth. Only three of them ("These Are the Subtle Rhythms," "The

Dream Was Mine," and "I, in My Pitiful Flesh") seem to bear a signature, and the last of these is marred at a crucial point by a formal lapse in which Wescott expresses the central joy of the poem as "On, oh . . ."[3] More than two thirds of the poems are the "black litanies" of youth: one group consists of the autumn or bittern poems in which "Autumn with her tale of losses" is used symbolically for the theme of melancholy; another of poems in which Wescott speaks sadly and despairingly through the persona of an old man; and the other of variations on the "after image" theme in which some fearful or melancholy residual memory "clings to the eye of thought" and, in one of the best metaphors in the book, makes it impossible for the poet "to walk/From May to May." Though it is not possible to question the authenticity of Wescott's melancholy, even despair —he attempted suicide in 1918 and was sick enough in 1919 to have to withdraw from the University of Chicago after only a year and a half there[4]—the poems which he wrote during this period strike one as poetic exercises in an assortment of melancholy postures in which, occasionally, one of the poems or some of the images show the self in attitudes which were to become characteristic and hence are part of the organic development.

"I, in My Pitiful Flesh" is such a poem, for its theme—the liberation of the flesh from the prison of guilt—is the central one in *The Apple of the Eye*. "These Are the Subtle Rhythms" is another such poem. The rhythms are those of "sloth," which is presented as the sensuous enjoyment of life for its own sake; they are subtle because they induce a laziness in the artistic self and keep it from creating. This conflict between the demands of life and the sense that one's destiny and hence one's duty is to work and create is recurrent in Wescott. And the "after image" theme—the prism (and prison) of memory—is not only one of the main themes of *The Grandmothers*, but another of the recurrent themes in all of his work. Finally, Wescott was later to use and caricature his own tendency toward such histrionic posturing in two of his best and most original fictional works: *The Babe's Bed* and *The Pilgrim Hawk*. This much, then, of *The Bitterns* is at least personally and organically important.

Natives of Rock is a much better book than *The Bitterns*; it has the same kind of relationship to *The Bitterns* that *The*

Pilgrim Hawk has to *The Babe's Bed,* for in each case the later
work completes and perfects the best dominant tendencies of
the earlier. It is with *Natives of Rock* that Wescott makes his
contribution to Imagist poetry and becomes significant, in a
minor way, in the history of poetry in the 1920's. His acknowl-
edged indebtedness in this book is to H. D. and Ezra Pound; his
earliest literary associations are with the Chicago *Poetry* group;
and such historical importance as these poems have comes from
the fact that in them Wescott brought to perfection two of
the "experimental forms of order" which Frederick J. Hoffman
lists in his discussion of Imagism. This list is arranged from
simple to complex and includes five "forms": "the first of these
is 'pure imagery,' with little or no attempt to 'intrude' a meaning upon an isolated imagistic statement"; the second " 'adds to'
or imposes upon the image an indication of attitude or an
external 'use' of imagery"; the third is what Hoffman calls the
"image cluster" and defines as "an accumulation of images, with
spatial and temporal orders of varying complexity"; the fourth
is the Imagistic poem which is "symbolic in an elementary sense"
because the images are clearly used as "symbolic 'tags' "; and
the fifth is "forms of symbolic order," where the whole poem
(for example, *The Waste Land*) is raised to the symbolic level
and depends for its order upon the manipulation of the symbols.[5]
It is with the first two "forms of order" that Wescott worked;
occasionally one of his poems seems to fit into the third or
"image cluster" group; but never do the poems rise to the fourth
and fifth orders. Most of the tags which Hoffman and others
quote from H. D. or Pound or even T. E. Hulme in their discussion of theoretical Imagism describe, with almost embarrassing
accuracy, most of Wescott's poems. This fit would suggest that
Wescott had the theory in his head and was working toward the
perfect realization of it in his poems; that he was consciously
writing a particular kind of poetry, deliberately experimental
and, at the time, very new. Again, as Hoffman and others point
out, pure Imagist poems are an extremely limited kind of poetry,
for the ostensibly "scientific" but ultimately unnatural goal is to
detach the "I" from the "eye" in order to produce an exact, that
is perspectiveless, image of the "thingness" of the object. The
reality is the unique object (rather than the observer, or the
experience of the object, as in Emily Dickinson), and the two

[27]

poetic vehicles are the senses, which apprehend the object, and words, which are used to throw back or reproduce the images and cadences (not the idea) of the object.

The ideal Imagist poem, to modify Mr. Ransom's now celebrated phrase, would be perfectly anonymous—all object and no self. The historical significance of Wescott's endeavors in poetry consists in the fact that in a small way he was part of this experiment and wrote a number of Imagist poems as nearly anonymous as any poems could be. It is precisely this point which leads to the organic and personal—and ultimately more important—significance of the poems, for the buried or unvoiced dialectic of Imagist poetry is the denial of self which the theory imposes on the poet. To succeed as an Imagist poet is to silence the voices of the self in order that the objects may speak through the neutralized perceiver. And objects, without an interpreting observer, speak an unusually bleak language. The suddenness and completeness with which Wescott dropped poetry, as well as the characteristic symbolic loading in his subsequent work by means of a fictional self (such as Alwyn Tower) or directly, by Wescott himself, in the essays, would suggest some sort of realization on Wescott's part that, though the lyric impulse was natural to him, Imagist poetry as a mode of expressing it was a kind of self-denial and alien to him as an artist. The conflict between the proper role of the self in art and its variants in life has bothered Wescott all of his creative life; in fact, it constitutes one of the recurrent agons in his work, and one of the agonies out of which he has made his art.

The poems in *Natives of Rock* are almost too easily discussed once one has come upon or figured out the formula in terms of which many of them were written and purged from one's mind the lingering doubts that they must mean and be more than they seem to. Many of them have a small perfection, both in themselves and as a particular kind of poem. Their range of subject, theme, and attitude is extremely narrow; the most severe technical limitations have been imposed upon them. Few lines or phrases, even after repeated readings, remain in the mind; and only a few of the poems can be remembered with the kind of pleasure that sends one back to them. The majority of the poems have a barren beauty which is inherent in the Imagist formula rather than in the poet. One has the sense that the poet has been refined out of existence, often unwillingly and at great pain. The collection, short as it is, has the monotony that seems to be inherent both in the formula and in its scrupulous application. Even the most minor variations are a welcome relief: sometimes there is a lapse into abstract meaning, as in "Magnolias and the Intangible Horse," when the horse is identified, within parentheses, as "nostalgia"; sometimes, as in the four "Mountain" poems, a succession of moments—the semblance of a plot—is used to give the reader something besides images to contemplate; and sometimes, as in "The Penitent in the Snow," the whole poem transcends the formula to become charged with meaning. But these are the exceptions: for the most part, the poems present what the eye has seen and the ear heard in a succession of precise visual and auditory images of natural phenomena. Occasionally (in six of the twenty poems) the "I" to which the eyes and ears belong is brought into the poem; and occasionally (in two of these six) the "I" is accompanied by another person. Ten of the poems are more or less pure observation of nature; four (the "Mountain" sequence) present a pattern of experience; four are observations of people, always in nature; one describes a funeral; and one clearly presents an interior experience of the "I" rather than what the eye has observed.

The collection is uniformly excellent in many ways: all the poems succeed as Imagist poems; there are none of the lapses into sentimentality which are so frequent in *The Bitterns;* and there is none of the posturing and little of the histrionic despair and melancholy of the first collection. The one persona through which Wescott speaks—in the "Mountain" sequence—is this time a young mountain shepherd, and the subject of the poem is loneliness, desire, and love. All the poems have a maturity about them; and, whether one likes them or not, they are experienced as poems rather than as juvenilia. Set against the poems in *The Bitterns,* those in *Natives of Rock* are a good example of how quickly and how early Wescott developed: he was twenty or twenty-one when he wrote them and twenty-four when he revised them for the book. In retrospect it seems perfectly clear that, had he wished, Wescott could have gone on to become a poet; there is no indication that he could not have mastered other poetic forms as quickly and thoroughly as he did Imagism. That he started with poetry is in itself significant, for his talent has always been essentially lyric, and in many ways his career is best understood as a life-long attempt to find a satisfactory way of expressing that talent in prose.

III

The book reviews Wescott wrote during this period may be regarded as the first of his experiments in prose, though in the strict sense they clearly represent a second means of entering directly into the literary life of the time, as well as a way of making some money. Wescott has always taken literature and the life of a professional man of letters with great seriousness; this characteristic integrity is seen in the reviews which, one must remember, are the work of a very young man. The reviews are in three groups: those done for *Poetry* (1921-22), for *The New Republic* (1923), and for *The Dial* (1923-25), plus one essay-review in 1925 which was written for *The Transatlantic Review*. The same kind of development which took place between *The Bitterns* and *Natives of Rock* can be seen in the progression from one review to another.

Wescott wrote four reviews for *Poetry* which, aside from their significance as his earliest published expository prose—and the prose really is remarkable when one remembers that Wescott was only twenty when he wrote the reviews—are chiefly interesting because they show a tendency exactly opposite to the one manifested in the Imagist poems. The tendency is toward truth-saying, toward statements in an epigrammatic or aphoristic style which are meant to set off reverberations of profundity. In one sense, these statements are not so opposite to the Imagist poems, for they are the parallels in the realm of abstractions to the precise visual and auditory images out of which the poems are made. But they are exactly opposite in the sense that Imagist poems, by intent, attempt to make no abstract statements. All of Wescott's reviews and, later, most of his essays, essay-reviews, and fictional works, are punctuated with such statements.

One of these statements appears in the first review Wescott ever wrote: "The individual talent," he said, "cannot develop richly without an historic sense" (*Poetry*, XVIII, 288). This is

announcement of a new intellect, acute and passionate, to scrutinize experience with an unfamiliar penetration and to substitute for it, as it ceases, new form and light." "What is done," he goes on to say, "is still; the memory can make these events a part of itself, but cannot turn them into a theory or a proposal" (LXXV, 282). Finally, as the highest kind of praise, he says that in her collection "the racial memory, the animal memory, has been strangely extended; and memory is the identifiable soul" (284). These remarks set the tone and indicate the intent of all the other reviews written for *The Dial*, including one in 1927 of a novel by Elizabeth Madox Roberts.

During this period, in addition to *The Dial* reviews, Wescott wrote and published "Bad Han" (1924); wrote two thematically related sequels to that story and published the whole as *The Apple of the Eye* (1924); wrote and published at least two of the stories ("In a Thicket," 1924, and "The Runaways," 1925) which later appeared in *Good-Bye Wisconsin;* began *The Grandmothers* (February, 1925); revised the poems which appeared in *Natives of Rock* (1925); and wrote "The Quarter's Books" piece which appeared in *The Transatlantic Review* (Autumn, 1925). It was an enormously productive and formative period, marked primarily by Wescott's rapid development as a writer of prose-fiction; and secondarily by his equally rapid development into a professional man of letters. The reviews which Wescott wrote during this period are an important part of both developments, for in them he theorized about prose-fiction specifically, and art generally, and about the nature and function of the artist, especially in the contemporary scene. In two of these reviews—those about Mary Butts and E. M. Roberts —he experimented with, or perhaps just fell into, the lyric essay, or essay-review which was later to become his characteristic, idiosyncratic mode of expression in expository or critical prose.

Wescott has always been an unusually self-conscious writer: introspective and subjective in the extreme. He is naturally inclined toward abstractions, theorizing, generalizing, and the making of aphorisms. These tendencies are clearly seen in *The Dial* reviews. The quotations from the review of Mary Butts, for example, especially the second, make such generalizations about art and prose-fiction. In this same review Wescott also says that "of all forms of utterance, narrative, the description of a mobile cluster of experiences, is the least easily comprehensible; the contrary appears to be true only because debased romancers [the prostitutes of art mentioned above] have too long imitated a redundant theatre" (LXXV, 283). Wescott begins a review of Marianne Moore's *Observations* with the assertion that "the world which surrounds us may be divided into two portions: that which we have experienced, and that which we have not—the latter a vague, tedious environment, an infinitude of things in which we have no interest." This opening categorical statement is followed by a chain of similar ones, the burden of which is that since "it is not possible to widen indefinitely the range of one's empiric knowledge of life," the "irreplaceable value of literature as culture" comes from the fact that it is "a form of vicarious living—for the reader, not for the writer" (LXXVIII, 1). Wescott's highest praise comes when he says that Miss Moore's real achievement is "not pure grace or clarity, but the self-portrait of a mind—to be appreciated, not as a model and not as beauty, but as an experience." Significantly enough, Wescott quotes John Dewey in this review and concludes it with some sonorous lines from Miss Moore's poem "In the Days of Prismatic Colour" to the effect that "Truth" is "no formal thing" and that the truth of Miss Moore's experiences will still " 'be there when the wave has gone by.' "

During this period, when he began so many of his own experiments in prose fiction, Wescott was clearly attempting to arrive at an idea of the novel and to formulate a theory about the relationship of art to experience. In a 1925 review of R. H. Mottram's *The Spanish Farm*, he restates one of the central ideas of the Marianne Moore review—that the function of art is "to expand the straitness of experience, and dispel the intolerance of the incurably lonely mind"—and then goes on to say that

> fiction has been an affair of personalities, of confidences which in life one dares not expect and scarcely dares to receive, of answers to the "why" which the slightest human action provokes. The world of the traditional novel is a world of faces, each of which, if seen in the street, would make one pause, and wonder, and perhaps follow the stranger a little way in the direction of his unknown purpose. Its beauty lies in the uniqueness of each object and each face, the precision of each colour, and the

radiance of each profile. The ideal novel, in this sense, would be like a tree whose every twig lies on the boughs in full relief—not even the smallest can unfold without rousing one's joy, or break and fall without producing sadness (LXXIX, 247).

Aside from the fact that this passage might serve as a description of what Wescott was doing in *The Grandmothers*, it is chiefly interesting as yet another statement of the recurrent idea in all of these reviews and in Wescott's criticism everywhere: that art—fiction in particular—must be an image of truth (reality) or it fails in its purpose. What the reviews make clear is that aside from the truth of images, as in *Natives of Rock* and all of Wescott's fiction, there is also the truth of statement: answers to the "why," knowledge of the "unknown purpose." This second kind of truth depends upon an observer-interpreter, someone who can both apprehend and present reality with the directness and accuracy of the Imagist poet and apprehend and present truth with the directness and accuracy of the aphorist. The ideal artist, whether poet, narrator, or dramatist, is the one who can combine image and truth in such a way as to present the fullest sense of reality. And, as I think the reviews make clear, Wescott felt that narrative—the novel—was the ideal art form because it allowed the maximum opportunity for presenting the fullest sense of reality.

In the final (1927) review of this period Wescott returns once more to these ideas. He begins the review of an Elizabeth Madox Roberts novel by saying that "roughly speaking, philosophy and character are the subjects of fiction." By philosophy he means the content of truth in the work and by character he means accurate portraiture—images not of nature, as in *Natives of Rock*, but of the self. "The poet's purpose," he says, is "to put the reader under a spell or a series of spells" (LXXXIII, 73). The object of the spellbinding is to compel the reader to truth, to a sense of reality; the writer does this, not only with his subject matter and themes, but with his style, by which he controls the tone of the work. The author, Wescott says, must bring to his work a "certain personal nobility" for the "least pusillanimity, the least vulgarity of over emphasis" would produce "grossness" and "nightmare" (75). Wescott is not speaking here of decorum but of the courage which the artist needs to confront the reality of experience directly, and of the integrity which the artist must have so that he will present the images and truths with the minimum of distortion.

All of these remarks place a terrible burden on the writer. When he dropped poetry and took up prose fiction, presumably because it allowed the maximum opportunity for presenting the fullest sense of reality and conveying the greatest amount of truth, Wescott assumed this burden, consciously and with great seriousness. His sense of his burden, which is sometimes extremely painful, is one of the keys to his development and to the particular qualities of all his work.

IV

Wescott's ideas of what art and the artist should be are again central themes in the essay which he wrote from New York in the autumn of 1925 for *The Transatlantic Review;* but in this essay he links these ideas to what can be called an expatriation complex of terms and thus provides one explanation of the significance of his eight-year sojourn in Europe which began in 1925. The essay is written in his attacking manner; the witty, ironic, and often brutal style he used in the *New Republic* reviews. A certain amount of what he says in *The Transatlantic Review* can be discounted for reasons of stylistic enchantment, but it would be foolish to discredit the whole essay simply because it glitters. To anyone familiar with the history of the 1920's, many of the things which Wescott says are more than stylistic tricks: they are brilliantly, often savagely, satiric. The burden of the essay is a great revulsion against the vulgarity, cultural aridity, and moral hypocrisy of American life, which are manifested in such things as prohibition and "His Censorship Mr. Sumner," but are attributable, ultimately, to "public opinion" (II, 446).

"In Kentucky, in New England, in the notorious Middle West, everywhere," Wescott says, "there is an Indignant Population which regards even the contents of *The Dial* with moral disgust, from whose viewpoint, indeed, all writing, except what is efficiently, professionally concocted to supply a demand, is an abomination" (447). Then, as in the *New Republic* reviews, Wescott goes after these "hacks," and always for the same two reasons: because they have prostituted their talent and betrayed the high calling of art; and because, as a result, they all suffer from "Kleig eyes, a blindness produced by the artificial light used in motion picture studios" (446). In such an America, Wescott says, "all [true] artists are spiritual expatriates. Their position in this commonwealth is that of a band of revolutionaries or a cult of immoralists. They exist by sufferance, by their willingness to endure poverty, or by 'protective colouration.'"

The artist in America *is* an expatriate, Wescott says; for this reason he contemplates with a good deal of irony the villainous epithets—"treason," "folly," "immorality"—hurled across the Atlantic at the actual expatriates by those who, at home, are "surrounded (and ignored) by the Indignant Population, hedged in (and boycotted) by the Professionals" (447). At the end of the essay, after passing references to Marianne Moore, William Carlos Williams, Wallace Stevens, and Yvor Winters as poets who are doing something new and worth while, Wescott says, with heavy intentional irony, that their works "are probably as well known in Paris as in New York" (448).

The implications here are clear enough: at one point in the essay Wescott says that the literary situation in America is really so dismal "it seems necessary to do something—to deliver a lecture, to commit suicide, to take the next boat to Paris" (447-48). Wescott took the "next boat to Paris," presumably because he could live there in a way that was better suited to his needs and because he could better fulfill his destiny as an artist. Recently, however, Wescott has said that he always loved America and went to Europe primarily because he could live there on what he made as a writer. That he always loved America is probably true; for, like Joyce, he wrote of almost nothing but his native land while he was in Europe.

But to say that he left his homeland only for economic reasons seems like a patent denial of the deep personal and artistic motives which must have impelled him toward Europe in the first place. There are more than economic motives involved in the prolonged eastward movement which characterizes Wescott's life for more than ten years and provides him with many of the major themes for much of his fiction. As Fred M. Millet has astutely pointed out, many of Wescott's reasons for going to Europe are to be found in the style and tone of *A Calendar of*

Saints for Unbelievers (1932), the last book he wrote in Europe and, as Millet says, the one which best "represents Wescott's most complete submission to sophisticated European influences."[6] The movement which is completed in *A Calendar of Saints for Unbelievers* (the last of six books written between 1924 and 1932) is begun in *The Apple of the Eye*; and, in a sense, neither that book nor any of the others can be understood properly or fully out of the context of Wescott's development as a writer and apart from the unusually close relationship that exists between his life, the place where he is living, and what he writes.

CHAPTER 2

The Bitter Apples, 1924

WESCOTT'S FIRST NOVEL was published in 1924 when he was twenty-three years old. It was begun, he indicates at the end, in 1918 in Kewaskum, Wisconsin (his birthplace), and completed in 1924 in New York City. Actually, as he says elsewhere, most of it was written between the summer of 1921 and the winter of 1923 after he had left the Midwest and started his eastern journey. The history of the novel's composition is interesting for it has led many critics to the conclusion that *The Apple of the Eye* is not a novel at all, but a set of three thematically related long stories. And this common misconception, along with the highly original form of *The Grandmothers,* has led most critics to conclude that Wescott is not really a novelist at all but primarily a writer of stories, which he puts together in a way that lacks some essential organic unity.[1] Neither of these works, however, lacks unity; as in so many modern novels—Joyce's *A Portrait of the Artist as a Young Man,* for example, which it seems to me Wescott consciously imitates—the unity derives from something other than a well-made plot.

All of Wescott's best work is essentially lyric, and the lyric novelist is under no compulsion to create in accordance with the accepted or traditional canons of the form. The whole Romantic movement freed the artist from that obligation by enabling him to use the individual self and the creative imagination as sources of unity. In one sense, the history of the modern novel, especially in England and America, is one of technical innovation, particularly in style, structure, and the manipulation of point of view as manifestations of a new idea of the self and the nature of reality. As Joseph Warren Beach and others have pointed out, Wescott has a place, albeit small, in that history;[2]

and, had he been able to discard some curiously fixed notion of what a narrative ought to be and follow his own genius, his place in that history would have been much larger, for he had (and still has) a highly original talent.

The Apple of the Eye is divided into three sections: "Bad Han," "Rosalia," and "Dan Alone." "Bad Han," which Wescott says he began in earnest in the summer of 1921 while living in the Berkshires, was written first as a long story and subsequently published in two parts in *The Dial* in 1924. When he had finished "Bad Han," Wescott says, "it occurred to me to extend the story into a novel" and to "show how such a person might have a good effect on her environment, as a kind of saint."[3] These extensions are in two parts, and the main indication that they were conceived after the "Bad Han" section is a minor confusion—very rare in Wescott—in the chronology. According to the facts given in Book I, Rosalia was born in 1891 or 1892 and would have been about eighteen at the time of Bad Han's death in 1910; but in Book II, Bad Han has clearly been dead for at least six years, which would make Rosalia twenty-four, and yet we are told that Rosalia is just "ready for Normal School," which would make her about eighteen (201).

This minor confusion is not so trivial as it probably seems, for it is a sign of the difficulty Wescott had in wedding the two bodies of material out of which he made the novel—the same two, incidentally, which he used in *The Grandmothers*. "Bad Han" is based, Wescott says, on an old family servant whose life he learned about from his mother.[4] "Rosalia" and "Dan Alone" are autobiographically based. The two parts of the novel come from different kinds of experience and different orders of time: the first is remote, semi-legendary, and apprehended by way of someone else's memory; the second is more immediate, non-legendary, and apprehended directly by the self. In some ways, the first body of material comes ready made for the young narrator of fictions: it is impersonal and already in the form of a tale; making a story out of it is essentially a problem in narration, a kind of technical exercise in which one uses already charged and partially shaped material.

But the second body of material is not ready made at all: to use it, one must find the legend in one's own life while it is still in tumultuous process. One must, in other words, re-create in the fiction the process that is actually going on in one's life—the brooding, involuting search for the form and meaning of one's self. Like most first novels and most novels written by very young authors, *The Apple of the Eye* is a fictional quest in which education, growth, and departure are the pivotal moments. The center of the novel and the primary source of unity is not really Bad Han, but Dan Strane (Wescott's first fictional disguise), who searched her legend and discovered a form and meaning in his own life. Bad Han and her marsh are the central positive symbols of the novel. Her legend is the exemplar, the saint's life, which is regional in origin but speaks ultimately in the universal language of the self.

This legend is presented first and functions as the narrative text for the sequence of anti-Puritan (in Van Wyck Brooks's sense of the term) sermons which are delivered in the rest of the novel. The significance of Bad Han lies in the fact that she transcended her region: she is an anti-Puritan saint of "life" because she knew that there was nothing to do with life but live it. In the first sequel, the "Rosalia" section, Mike Byron is Bad Han's spiritual son and the first of the anti-Puritan preachers or teachers who educate Dan Strane and finally liberate him from the evasion of experience by theory which his mother, the church, and region in general advocate. Jules Bier—Dan's uncle, and, in his youth, Bad Han's lover—is the second major anti-Puritan preacher and teacher: he delivers the decisive sermon to Dan at the end of the book, which is simply the telling and searching of Bad Han's legend. Dan's third preacher and teacher is Bad Han herself; for, after hearing her legend, he becomes not only her spiritual son but also her disciple. The first time he preaches the gospel—relates Bad Han's legend—to Mrs. Dunham, he encounters the last of his teachers and the third of his "mothers" in the novel. In telling the story to Mrs. Dunham, Dan discovers his twin vocations: to apprehend "life" and to convey it, or the sense of it, in art. Dan's early education and initial growth to manhood are now complete and all that remains is departure from the home and region in order that he might go about his "business," which, like the "purpose" of "life," "was to go on, just to go on" (279, 280).

The significance of the three mothers and all the teachers is that each gave Dan "life" in one form or another. In one sense, the two male teachers are also his mothers, for the term is used here, as in *The Grandmothers*, metaphorically, to indicate that the self is born of many mothers, including, in a kind of metaphorical incest, itself. The "awakening" of the self to life, like the initial physical parturition, is a separation of the part from the whole, a necessary severing. Much of the novel is concerned with Dan's separation from his actual mother, his family, his home, his Puritan heritage, his region, his childhood—all the cords which must be severed if the self is to awaken and have a life of its own. The theme of the novel is the reversed Genesis myth which is so common in modern literature and an obsessive recurrent theme in all the other anti-Puritan literature of the period in America.[5] The myth is reversed by making the bitter apples of experience the food of the self; if there is to be life, the self must pick and eat the apples. Not to pick and eat—to obey the commandments referred to on the title page in the quotation from Proverbs—is to evade experience by theory, to starve the self to death. Or, as in the case of Rosalia, to eat (she never willingly picked) while still under a compulsion to obey the commandments, is ultimately to be destroyed by a death-dealing theory: she commits suicide in Bad Han's marsh in the dead of winter after an affair with Mike Byron, paralyzed by fear and guilt, and under the ironic delusion that she is pregnant—that there is life in her. She dies, in one of the fine paradoxical metaphors of the novel, a virgin mother.

The agon in the novel is between life and death, and it takes place primarily within the self of Dan Strane, who by the end has been educated to the point where he escapes Rosalia's fate (victimization by the regional Puritanism) and is delivered to the unknown promises of life. At the time when this novel was published (1924), there was nothing very radical about this theme; and, as is often true of first books by young authors, there is not too much that is original about *The Apple of the Eye* as a novel. Like the comparable first fruits of Wescott's equally precocious contemporaries—F. Scott Fitzgerald and James Gould Cozzens, who had novels published at twenty-four and twenty-one, respectively—*The Apple of the Eye* is imitative and has many of the shortcomings of most such youthful works: tonal lapses, stylistic failures, a profusion of descriptive set pieces, unrealized characters, and thematic pedantries.

To treat the novel as a mature work is unjust: it is not the creation of a developed novelist but an initial attempt in a new form and medium: an exploration of the possibilities of prose fiction after a similar exploration in poetry. As such, it is especially significant because it represents the form Wescott settled on: since the mid-1920's, for example, even though he has published in a great variety of other forms, he has never thought of himself as anything but a novelist. Moreover, like *The Bitterns* and the early reviews, which are its poetic and prose counterparts in Wescott's development as a writer, *The Apple of the Eye* is an early work in which all the arrows point forward. "Bad Han," for example, points toward the later regional stories collected in *Good-Bye Wisconsin;* and the novel as a whole points toward *The Grandmothers*, in which much of the material and many of the themes are reworked—but this time in a highly original form. And, finally, *The Apple of the Eye* is Wescott's first tentative attempt to work out in practice the theory of the novel—actually of art—that is stated and developed in all his reviews of the 1920's. The tentativeness must be stressed, for there is a profusion of non-functional images in the work which is clearly a carry-over from the Imagist period; the novel is also filled with baldly stated truths; and the narrative thread upon which the images and truths are strung is inadequate. Wescott had not yet perfected either the first-person or limited third-person point of view which would permit the use of a viewing, interpreting, truth-saying, participating narrator, or the techniques of lyric fiction which would enable him to synthesize and make organically functional the images and truths without benefit of the traditional plot.

In spite of its faults, *The Apple of the Eye* is an impressive first novel for a twenty-three-year-old. The failures are mostly those of an apprentice; as such, they are not failures of talent but those which result from lack of experience, inadequate training in the craft of fiction, and insufficient knowledge. The chief failures, for example, are in the dialogue, in the characterizations of all but Dan Strane, and in most of the explicit thematic passages or conversations in books II and III. The three worst and most damaging failures are Mike Byron and all the scenes in which he is involved; Rosalia, especially in her mad scenes; and the episode in Book III where Dan's uncle

Jules sums up the theme of the novel. These failures are all of a piece, for they are all manifestations of Wescott's inability at this stage in his development to translate his truths into fictional terms. Mike Byron, Jules Bier, and Rosalia are failures because they are not characters at all but ideas or attitudes with names attached to them. They have a reality as ideas or attitudes but at the level of plot, action, and character—at the level of fiction and invention where the idea must be filled out and particularized in terms of character—they have little or no reality. As a result, almost all of Book II—Rosalia's and Mike Byron's book, really—is a failure; the only things which redeem it are Dan Strane, whose education and growth begin here, and the exact details of the regional scene and the life there.

The often brilliantly realized realities in this novel are Bad Han's legend, Dan Strane, and the regional scene. When he deals with these three subjects, Wescott is nearly faultless, for they have compelled his imagination to the point where he can write of them from knowledge and in the rapt, spellbinding way that is characteristic of all his best work. When Wescott takes up the interior life of Dan Strane's self—his inward explorations, his memories, his reveries, his experience of things, even his melodramatic and adolescent agonies—the novel takes on a life that it does not have elsewhere. This is because Wescott is here writing the first chapter of his fictional autobiography, searching, as it were, his own adolescence for the universal legend of the self which he feels is implicit in his own experience.[6]

This experience is so completely and intimately bound up with the region and all that goes with it that the two cannot be separated, which is why the region here and in *The Grandmothers* has such power and vitality, even though, in both books, it is rejected, painfully, and then only after the most scrupulous and excruciating kind of meditation upon its nature and significance. Finally, the telling of Bad Han's legend comes from the same source of compulsion. She provides the answer to the riddle of the inscrutable region: if one is to avoid Rosalia's fate—her "unresolved Puritanism" kills her[7]—one must search out the bitter apples, pick and eat them willingly and without remorse. When he brings Dan Strane to this realization near the end of the novel, when he has gone full circle from Bad Han's legend to the legend implicit in Dan Strane's adolescence, Wescott has discovered and presented the universal legend of the self which was implicit in his own regional experience.

Wescott has, in other words, found the form, subjects, and themes which were to be his sole concern for the next six years until, apparently, he felt that he had exhausted the subjects and themes and could go no further with the form until he discovered, again only after a long, slow growth in the womb of memory, other universal legends implicit in his own experience as an expatriate, artist, and man.

CHAPTER 3

The Native Land of the Imagination, 1925-1927

I

LIKE MOST of his fictional heroes, Wescott was always saying good-bye and departing. Between 1920 and 1933, Wescott's life, like that of so many others during this period, was characterized by a great restlessness. He was always going somewhere: the two recurrent metaphors are of the mother—that to which one is attached and from which one must depart—and of the journey. Unlike Fitzgerald, whose sad chronicle is the interminable succession of hotels at which he and Zelda stayed,[1] Wescott usually worked out of relatively fixed locations—Chicago, New York, Paris, Villefranche, and again Paris—until he returned to America for good in 1933 and settled first in New York and then, in 1943, in the family enclave in New Jersey.

While he was living in America, Wescott journeyed frequently to Europe: after he had moved to Europe, he returned periodically to his actual and metaphorical mothers in Wisconsin. Even when he was not making the physical journey, he wandered through his memories of Wisconsin, his family, and America; out of these he made all of the fictions which he wrote during this period. Thus, though he was actually living in Europe as an expatriate, Wescott's imaginative and creative life was lived in Wisconsin, and his creative efforts were directed toward the re-creation and searching of his familial, regional, and national origins. Much of Wescott's fiction during this period is reconstructed history: memory provides the facts, the imagination apprehends and adds to them, and some searching faculty of the self—fictionally embodied in Alwyn Tower or his equivalent—meditates toward the truth of history as memory and imagination have re-created it. The results are not history in the usual sense, but historical fictions or fictional histories which, like history, preserve the past for its own sake and search it to find the truth it contains for the present.

Between 1925 and 1930 Wescott published three books of historical fictions, all of them regional in the sense that each is based on the Wisconsin material. They, along with *The Apple of the Eye,* constitute Wescott's total output as a so-called Midwestern regional writer. After 1930 he never published any more regional fiction, and he seldom used his Midwestern experiences in any of his writing. That chapter of his own history was finished: he had exhausted it as a source of images and had discovered all of the truth which it contained for him. It is as if, after *The Babe's Bed* (which is like a late child, and was in fact the result of his last visit to Wisconsin), he had said "finished." Unlike Faulkner, who compulsively rewrote most of his fictional histories until he had raised them to the level of redemptive myth and fable, literally reconstructing a South he could not leave in fictions he could rewrite at will, Wescott said good-bye to the region once and for all and departed.[2] It was to his mother, family, and native land that he later returned, not to the Midwest.

II

As early as 1916, while he was still in high school, Wescott had left home; by 1919, he had left Wisconsin; by 1921, he had left the Midwest; and, by 1925, he had left America. The first of these departures is the subject of *The Apple of the Eye* and the whole sequence is the subject of *The Grandmothers.* The principal difference between the two novels is reflected in the nature of the departures with which both novels are brought to a close. Dan Strane's is a natural late adolescent departure from a very specific place, from childhood, from the family, and from all that is familiar and known. But Alwyn Tower's departure is much more inclusive and has a finality about it that is beyond the experience and knowledge of Dan Strane. Alwyn Tower narrates the novel in retrospect from Europe, re-creating from memory the chronicle of his family and region in order that he may meditate on it and in this way exorcise (not rationalize) the powerful spell which both still have on him. Only a fragment of the novel takes place in the fictional present; all the rest is after the fact: the departures have all been made at the level of reason and physical action; but, like memory, the spell is residual and part of the substance of the incurably remembering mind. The enchantment is *in* the memory and haunts it like an incubus; the memory in turn haunts the self which had thought that reason and physical action were enough. In order to go forward—to fulfill, that is, the destiny of Dan Strane, which is directly to confront and experience "life"— the spell has to be broken. The way to do this is to call up those things which have cast the spell and to confront them as a means of dissipating their power, which is exactly what Alwyn Tower does in *The Grandmothers*.

The novel has as its subtitle *A Family Portrait*, which indicates where the locus of the memory is. Early in the novel Alwyn Tower decides that "he had no native land—he had a family instead" (30). The family, individually and collectively, is systematically raised to higher and higher levels of generalization in the course of Alwyn Tower's long and loving journey through the known and invented facts of his memories until the family, its history, and the region have been charged with specifically American meanings and everything that is said about them is understood in a double sense. The Tower men, including Alwyn, are spoken of early in the novel as "perpetual pioneers" (30); they are all presented as pilgrims of the spirit whose lives tell over and over again what Wescott in *The Babe's Bed* called "a melancholy fantasy upon western themes" (8). The Towers, after their westward journey, from England first, and then from New York to Wisconsin, settle in a place which is later named "Hope's Corner." The significance of this name is given in an essay on America and his family which Alwyn is supposed to have written when he was nineteen:

> *Meanwhile the colonists had moved and moved again, from east to west, into every corner of the continent; and each migration repeated, with a little less religion and a little more weariness, the pilgrimage which had brought them there: disappointed men going further, hoping still . . .*
>
> *At last there was no corner where wealth and joy might be thought to dwell, no riverbed without a city, no empty valley,*

*no more coasts. At last those pilgrims who had failed to dis-
cover their hearts' desire had to look for it in heaven, as it had
been in Europe, as it had always been. Disillusioned but imaginative, these went through the motions of hope, still pioneers*
(28-29).

The stories of the Towers, which make up the composite
family portrait, are all American stories; and the subject of
The Grandmothers is the meaning of his American family to
Alwyn Tower. The movement of meaning in the novel is from
the individual to the type, from a family to the representative
American family, from a region to the nation, and from the
individual self of the narrator to Alwyn Tower as a representative American self. What makes this movement possible is
Alwyn Tower, from whose limited third-person point of view
the novel is narrated.

As Chapter II—"Alwyn's Knowledge of America and his
Family"—makes clear, there are three centers in this novel, all
identified in the chapter title: the Tower family and its history;
America; and Alwyn Tower as a member of the family, as a Mid-
westerner, as an American, and as a separate entity. Chapter II
and Chapter XV—"Conclusion"—also make clear that the novel
is essentially Alwyn's self-exploration in terms of his own and
his family's history and that the end result, as in all of Wescott's
novels, is to be truth, particularized here in the images of the
family and generalized in the conclusions that Alwyn arrives
at about himself, his family, and America. Chapter II is the
only place in which the fictional present of the novel is
identified: Europe is Alwyn's tower, the heaven he hoped for in
his childhood. He is, appropriately enough, always in a high
place when one sees him in Chapter II: first in the Austrian
Alps, and then on a terrace high above Monte Carlo. Europe is
his tower because in one sense it represents exactly the opposite
of what all the earlier westward-moving Towers had hoped for.
The Towers as a family settled in the Midwest at a geographical
place which was symbolically only a corner of hope—or at which
hope was always just around the corner. Many Towers subsequently went west, but they always returned to the Midwest.
By reversing this movement, Alwyn hopes to break the "griev-
ance" that was every Tower's "birthright" (32) as a "perpetual

pioneer" (30) and to end the "melancholy fantasy upon western themes" which his family and Americans in general have told over and over again. This is the central truth contained in the Towers' composite family portrait and chronicle.

Alwyn's prize—or, following the pun-logic in his name, the all that he will win when he has climbed the tower—is not Heaven or even the ironic prize of failure which most Towers win; his prize is separate selfhood and the destiny of Dan Strane, which is simply to live life. The first prerequisites are the three separations—from the family, from the region, from the nation—which Alwyn Tower has already effected. Hence the great importance of Europe and the fact that the novel is actually set there and is delivered as a long meditative memory sequence, part fact and part fiction, from that symbolically charged eastern-most place. But one can leave all of these things, as Wescott himself had begun to do as early as 1917, without ever actually relinquishing them. "After he had left home," Alwyn Tower thinks, from his vantage point in Europe,

> when most of his older relatives were dead, certain things of which he had remained in ignorance had continued to trouble him. For the personages in rocking-chairs, the questionable spirits leaning over his cradle, had embodied not only the past, but the future—his own wishes and fears; and he was not to be content until an everyday light had unveiled all their faces. To bring an end to his childhood, to drive its ignorance out of his heart, to conduct or try to conduct his own life in its alarming motion, he had been obliged to lead in imagination many lives already at an end. Now and again the riddle of his own experience had resembled one of the past's riddles; his personal solutions had solved them as well. Spell after spell had been lifted. He had been possessed by a family of spirits —now at last they were exorcised; and in their place there was this family of stories which he could not have remembered, but seemed nevertheless to remember (23-24).

The transformation of the "family of spirits" into a "family of stories" is what finally enables Alwyn Tower to relinquish all of these things by transcending them. The enabling factor is knowledge—the "everyday light"; more specifically, when he has read the meaning out of—or, sometimes, working from his own experience, back into—the individual lives of the spirits possessing him and given the whole the unity of a family, he has transformed each spirit into a portrait-story and the whole into the family portrait-chronicle which makes up the novel. These stories Alwyn describes as being "like a series of question marks; questions which did not require an answer, questions at peace." And he says that "he was content with their ambiguities, so he knew that they were the end of understanding, or at any rate, the end of trying to understand" (33).

Alwyn's tower, then, is also the ascent to knowledge; for it is this knowledge, along with the creative and re-creative process, which allows him to lay to rest the spirits that haunt his memory and imagination and to "conduct his own life in its alarming motion." What one tends to forget in reading *The Grandmothers* is that Alwyn's movements of perception are the true center of this lyric novel. The originality of the novel is not in its subject matter, and certainly not in its ideas about America,[3] but in its form. The technical advance from the frequently awkward and largely conventional *The Apple of the Eye* to the fluent, wonderfully controlled and highly original *The Grandmothers* is as astonishing in its own way as the technical advance from Fitzgerald's *This Side of Paradise* to *The Great Gatsby*.

In both cases, the use of a participating first-person or limited third-person narrator as a structural device is in part responsible for the originality and effectiveness of the form. The mind of the narrator, once it has established a point of view (in the non-technical sense) in what is the fictional present of the novel (Alwyn in Europe; Nick Carraway back in the Midwest), functions like a time machine: the whole novel issues from the mind of the narrator in non-chronological order, with the narrator sometimes functioning simply as a camera-eye or, in the most literal sense, as a narrator, and sometimes as a commentator and interpreter. Since the narrator both tells and participates in the story, and in both cases tells it after it has happened, when he is in another place and removed from it by time, he can comment from his present point in time, he can reproduce his own comments or reactions as he made or experienced them at any point in the actual chronology of events, he can make later comments on his own earlier ones, and he can judge and rejudge his earlier self as his later self sees it.

Wescott was to use this technique much more effectively and

thoroughly in *The Babe's Bed* and, later, with greater originality and power, in *The Pilgrim Hawk;* but he does use it first in *The Grandmothers*, and the importance of it to an understanding and appreciation of that novel, as well as of Wescott's development as a writer, can hardly be overestimated. In the most literal sense, the whole novel issues from Alwyn's mind; memory is his time machine and what drives him back into and then through these memories is his own search for knowledge and understanding. The novel is partly organized in terms of story-portraits, which are arranged in what appears to be a loose chronological order determined by the date of birth of the various members of the Tower family. The gradual over-all movement is from past to present. But, as in any novel narrated retrospectively from a limited third-person point of view and moved forward, as this one is, by a search for knowledge and understanding, time is always fluid and the movement through time is free and never essentially chronological. Many structural principles are at work in this novel, but the chief one—that which, contrary to what many critics have said, makes this a novel and not a collection of short stories—is Alwyn Tower as narrator.

Everything in the novel is related to Alwyn, just as children are to their parents; the Tower family produced Alwyn, but in Alwyn's meditations this relationship is reversed and the organic metaphor of the family is used to describe the relation between Alwyn and the story-portraits which make up the bulk of the novel. In an androgynous metaphor that is fairly common with artists, Alwyn is both male and female, but more mother than father; the story-portraits that issue from him are his family; the novel as a whole is his fictional child.[4] Everything that contributed to the making of the novel is brought in and included in the organic metaphor; and in the extraordinary conclusion to the novel, the same organic metaphor is used interchangeably to describe the creation of the novel and the birth, growth, and maturation of Alwyn's present self.

The title of this novel, in other words, especially the root-word —mother—is used metaphorically and then symbolically as it was in *The Apple of the Eye* to mean "that which had produced one" (364). The passion in this book is to know and understand. "The desire to understand," Alwyn points out, "was, after all, desire," and "curiosity was a child's love" (364). The passion leads to

many kinds of love, all of which, within the metaphor, are incestuous: for his family, his region, his nation are all metaphorical
mothers, grandmothers. Actually, Wescott's involuting mind has
made it a double incest, for Alwyn had loved them all as he grew
up "with the fever of inquisitiveness of an adolescent about love"
(366); and he loves them all again, in memory, so that "memory"
also is "incest" (378).

But the love, incestuous or not, "had been true love, and not
altogether sterile, illusory as the relation had been" (366). There
were two offspring, both of which are included within the
complex sexual-familial metaphor. The first child is described in
the following passage from the conclusion to the novel:

> In imagination, as adolescent boys, night after night and one
> indoor afternoon after another, suffer the enjoyment of those
> whom they have never touched or never even seen—he [Alwyn]
> also had exhausted his boyhood to master an abstraction, a
> wilderness in the abstract, and to wring from its hypocritically
> rich body—what? Just enough knowledge to live on. . . . And it
> was the mother of the weak, incalculable manhood which, within
> and protected by his immature arms, lay like a newborn child
> (366-67).

The "knowledge" which Alwyn "gained by breaking the law"
(365) makes possible the birth of this second self—the tower
above the Towers, Alwyn as a separate entity in Europe who is
able to lead an "entire life" (387). Alwyn's knowledge of his
family, his region, and his nation is the mother of his manhood,
and that child is the fruit of a passionate, incestuous love.

The "family of stories" which makes up the novel is fathered
by this first "child" out of memory and imagination. The novel
is not just a feat of memory: it is an act of love, as passionate
as the first; and it attests to the "wealth and power" of Alwyn
Tower's "patrimony" (368). The novel is an account of how
Alwyn's second self came to be born; it is the fictional genealogy,
with elaborate commentary, of this new self. As such, it is not
so much a portrait of the Tower family as it is Alwyn's self-
exploration and self-portraiture in terms of his family. If at times
certain of the story-portraits seem detached from Alwyn,
especially in the first half of the novel, it is only because one
has forgotten that originally in Alwyn's childhood and adoles-

cence perception was amplified by invention and passed into memory in this compounded form. Later, wherever his passion to know and understand was unsatisfied, he imaginatively created the facts and supplied the meanings, frequently using his own experiences and solutions to solve some of the "past's riddles" (24). Thus, though the novel is clearly autobiographical, Alwyn Tower is not Glenway Wescott and the novel is not history. Perhaps it should be called fictional history or symbolic autobiography. The novel is an almost classic example of the way in which the individual imagination has shaped and amplified a mass of facts in order to extract meaning from them. The end toward which the whole novel moves is usable knowledge; fiction becomes a mode of knowing and a means of conveying the truth.

The novel, for example, is punctuated by a series of reverberating generalizations, many of which are concentrated in the three Alwyn sections: Chapter II, the second half of Chapter XI (235-57), and Chapter XV. The generalizations—the body of abstract and particular truths which Alwyn Tower has been able to extract from the material—are the linking devices: the means by which each individual Tower is joined to the Tower family; the Towers as a whole to the pilgrims, Puritans, and pioneers; and the whole regional and family chronicle to the history of America. Almost without exception, every truth about the Towers, individually and collectively, is converted into a generalization about Americans and America.

Actually, there are three main bodies of truth, or more precisely, three kinds of truths in terms of which Alwyn conducts his self-exploration and works out his own self-portrait. These are what Alwyn calls the "materials" of his life or self which have been "determined in advance": "certain human limitations, American characteristics, family traits" (369). The movement of perception in the novel is back and forth between these three centers of knowledge, with the movement always controlled by Alwyn's "passion of curiosity" and compulsion toward usable knowledge (369).

These truths constitute the themes of the novel, the so-called universal truths at which all good writers working with regional material ultimately arrive. Love, for example, is one of these themes: love as a "trap" (289), lovers as fools (296), love as helpless (297), love as "madness" (298), love and passion as insatiable, incurable appetites (291) which lead only to loneliness (291), frustration, and sorrow. In fact, there are more aphorisms about love in this novel than about almost anything else; only the Towers as hopeless idealists inspire more, and they are lovers all. At one point, Alwyn says that the family birthright is "anxiety, ambition, and loneliness" (246). Almost all of the Towers portrayed in the book are victims of "hopeless ambitions" (381), some "native land of their imagination" which is always just around the corner (375); and almost every Tower is love's victim, love's fool—whether by his own doing, or as a result of chance, fate, or some other cause. Like Alwyn's grandfather Tower, almost every other Tower either briefly possesses or glimpses his Serena only to lose her almost immediately and work out the rest of his life in helpless anxiety and loneliness. The novel is a chronicle of such failures: of perpetual pioneers who never get where they were going; of toppled towers; of generation after generation of men and women who helplessly, incurably, climb their towers in hope's corner to find the native land of their imaginations, their Serenas.

It is on this point and in the "Conclusion" to the novel that all the truths converge, for this is precisely the destiny which Alwyn is attempting to escape; and it is, he discovers, an American and an individual as well as a family destiny. He has won his way to a knowledge of what produced him (all his mothers, male and female, natural, regional, and national, as far back as memory will take him), and he has discovered the "human limitations," the "American characteristics," and the "family traits" of which he is composed. The question now is how these will combine in him, "one interrupting another, one melting into another," and the kind of "rhythm and order" that the combinations will give to his life (369). Alwyn hopes—and the word here as everywhere in the novel is heavily ironic—with the knowledge won to make his life resemble "a fugue, without a break (that is, without disaster) from beginning to end, without violent emphasis, each element in perfect relief, played without loss of memory or unsteadiness in either hand" (370). And he hopes further that his own life will be a "counterpoint of their [the family's] appetites, their frugality, cunning, vanity, idealism, and homesickness" (370).

Here the attitude which prevails throughout the novel toward America, Wisconsin, and the Tower family is re-expressed: this is not, after all, a novel about matricide; incest is the figure that prevails at the end, and it is a metaphor drawn from the love cluster which surrounds every Tower in the novel. Alwyn, like all the other Towers, is a victim of love; his love has been a "passion of curiosity" about his mothers, an "amorous effort to have the truth naked of its disguises, to reach the point where mortal desire leaves off and serene, immortal satiety begins"[5] (250-51). This passion was his ambition; it caused anxiety enough and, at the end, the loneliness of separation from all his mothers. But it also left him free; the love has apparently run its course, been purged now, a second time, out of the memory. Alwyn is left in his tower, with new knowledge and the hope that he will be able to leave—or is it escape?—the native land of his imagination and lead an "entire life."

CHAPTER 4

The Last Good-byes, 1928-1930

I

IN MANY WAYS it is unfortunate that the regional and historical content of *The Grandmothers* has been stressed so heavily, to the exclusion of its other qualities as a novel, as a highly original experiment in prose-fiction and as a work about love. These days, unjustly, it is relegated to a footnote or is treated in a few tiresomely repeated and not very accurate or useful sentences which cite it as a regional work belonging to the "revolt from the village" and the "criticism of American life" class of novels. Of course, these things are true of the novel. As early as 1932, Joseph Warren Beach pointed out that

> In Alwyn's reflections at the death-bed of his grandmother he sounds many notes in that criticism of American life which has taken on such volume in our letters since Van Wyck Brooks and Masters' "Anthology." Throughout this history what impresses him is the abortive idealism of these strenuous lives, the fundamental melancholy deliberately ignored, the fanatical Puritanism, the spiritual pride and failure.[1]

Anyone who has read Brooks's *America's Coming-of-Age*, or Paul Rosenfeld's wonderful essay on Brooks in *Port of New York,* or more recently, Sherman Paul's composite definition and discussion of the myth of America in the 1920's,[2] will recognize immediately the extent to which Wescott—like Fitzgerald, Rosenfeld, Hart Crane, and many others—embodied this "cultural myth" in his novel. The myth was a commonplace among American writers in the 1920's, especially among those associated with such magazines as *The Dial* and directly involved, as Wescott was, in the last stages of the artistic and intellectual renaissance which had begun around 1912. As Sherman Paul has shown, in his introduction to *Port of New York* as well as in his *Louis Sullivan: An Architect in American Thought*,[3] and as the whole of Rosenfeld's *Port of New York* demonstrates, the component parts of this myth were part of the intellectual atmosphere of the time. Even the expatriates—and maybe these more than any others—had taken this myth into their systems.

To read *The Grandmothers* in conjunction with the works mentioned above—and with *The Great Gatsby*—is to feel the full force of Sherman Paul's assertion that this myth was everywhere: the same phrases and ideas appear in all these works, often in such a way that they can be lifted out of one work and put into another without any loss of meaning or change of voice. It is probably no longer possible to tell who read whom; what one is left with are the astonishing similarities: a continuity that suggests a homogeneity beyond the wildest dreams of American litanists and culturologists.

Most of the male Towers, for example, are James Gatzes (living in Wisconsin instead of North Dakota) who yearn to become Jay Gatsbys, to spring newborn from the platonic conception of themselves. They are all would-be aristocrats of the imagination, perpetual pilgrims and pioneers, always ready to set sail by ship or prairie schooner for the fresh green breast of the new world of their imaginations. They live in a perpetual hope's corner, the fallen and frustrated idealists of the new world who are unable to "renounce the 'dream,'" "the voyage of yearning," "'the divine delusion.'"[4] When Brooks speaks of America as an "impoverished civilization" in which things were "old without majesty, old without mellowness, old without pathos, just shabby and bloodless and worn out,"[5] it might just as well be Alwyn Tower in one of his meditations on the condition of America—or Wescott himself speaking in the essay "Good-Bye Wisconsin." But there seems little point in simply documenting these similarities of idea, of phrase, and, more significantly, of style and tone; the important fact is that the myth, which is inherently powerful, was pervasive and that Wescott's use of it, which was certainly profound and carefully thought out, places the novel in a significant and deeply rooted American tradition.

But, just as Fitzgerald's use of these same ideas does not—in fact, cannot—account for the extraordinary power and originality of *The Great Gatsby*, Wescott's use of them cannot account for *The Grandmothers*. In many ways, love as a subject and theme is more central in *The Grandmothers* than America, just as the nature and sad—even tragic—destiny of the romantic self in the grip of a great tawdry dream is more central in *The Great Gatsby* than the specifically American setting and themes in terms of which Fitzgerald localized the story. Without forcing, it can be said of both these novels that they are, in Wescott's phrase, "melancholy fantasies upon western themes"; but western themes have never been the private property of the American imagination, though many of the greatest American works have been written on them. Just as one must perceive the ways in which Fitzgerald and Faulkner transcend their regional and American material, so one must see those things in Wescott if one is to get him out of the regional bin into which he was thrown many years ago. Faulkner's technical achievements are so overpowering that there has never really been any danger of the critics' putting him into a regional bin and leaving him there. The same is true of Fitzgerald: *Gatsby* keeps breaking out of the possessive embrace of the culturologists, and *Tender is the Night* beats out so sad and dark a rhythm that no purely historical or cultural approach could possibly encompass it.

My intention is not to raise *The Grandmothers* to the level of these works but to put it and Wescott's other regional works into an adjusted perspective. With his usual perceptiveness, Joseph Warren Beach pointed out (in 1932!) that in *The Grandmothers* Wescott

> has more the method of Conrad. Alwyn has somewhat the rôle of Marlow or Captain Mitchell. Like Conrad, Wescott likes to insist on the fragmentariness of his information, on the need for imaginative reconstruction; he makes great use of retrospection; he weaves back and forth in time. In some chapters he works in several periods simultaneously, deliberately interchanging distinct planes, in the modernistic manner.[6]

This is the first adjustment which needs to be made. What Beach says of *The Grandmothers* is also true of at least half the material in *Good-Bye Wisconsin*, including the title essay; and it

GLENWAY WESCOTT

is also true of *The Babe's Bed*, the last of the regional works and the most "modernistic" of them all. The technique which Beach describes is that of the lyric novel, an essentially Romantic and almost exclusively modern form. And this is the form of all of Wescott's best work—including his essays. It is his natural, organic form; working within it, he has experimented boldly, brilliantly, often achieving original and stunning results. This, then, would be the second adjustment, one that goes beyond purely technical matters—the "modernistic manner"—to a higher level where form is a manifestation of the self and an indication of concerns that transcend region and nationality. At this level, form becomes part of the universal language of the self.

The third adjustment would also be at the level of technique, and would be a matter of seeing more clearly the rich metaphorical and symbolic texture of the regional works. Wescott is a natural symbolist; the two characteristic movements of his mind are toward a profusion of specific concrete images and toward dense symbolism—almost a jungle of abstractions and generalizations. His mind moves with uncommon readiness from things to meanings, almost automatically converting things, places, people, events, and actions into private symbols. When this process works, the result is a rich concentration of meaning; when it does not work, as in some of the stories in *Good-Bye Wisconsin*, the result is dense evocation without resolution, which frustrates and annoys the cognitive part of the mind.

The fourth and final adjustment necessary for seeing Wescott's regional works as something more than regional portraits and historical statement is in the area of themes. Wescott's central subject and theme from *The Apple of the Eye* (1924) on is certainly not America or the Midwest, but love and the self. His conception of love is so purely Romantic that often the settings of his stories are purely coincidental. However, it is not quite accurate to say that he writes only of Romantic love, for love in all its variations is his central subject; and he has even used love metaphorically, as in *The Grandmothers*, to describe his own and his characters' passion to know. As in the work of D. H. Lawrence, love is always directly related to the self; in fact, Wescott hardly ever writes of the self apart from love. His best work, *The Pilgrim Hawk*, has as its subtitle *A Love Story*. In a sense, all of his fictional works and many of the non-fictional ones are also love stories: the single, most pervasive metaphor in *Fear and Trembling* is a sexual one, and love is an obsessive concern at every point in that book. Even *A Calendar of Saints for Unbelievers* has love and sexuality for a theme, for it is a witty and sophisticated compilation of brutalities, perversions, and stupidities, as well as more healthy acts, performed or suffered for the love of God, or some other deity.

With the help of these four adjustments, it is possible to see Wescott's regional fictions more clearly for what they are. To be sure, the two novels, stories, and the essay are regional, specifically Midwestern; they are also essentially American and deal with the American experience and the experience of being an American at home and in Europe; they are, for the most part, the work of an expatriate and thus belong to a significant and large body of work written by other expatriates during the same period about the same things. But they are more than any of these classifications; to lose sight of these other things would be an error of perception and judgment—and certainly an injustice to Wescott as a writer.

II

Good-Bye Wisconsin includes ten stories plus the title essay. The earliest work, by date of publication, is "In a Thicket," which first appeared in *The Dial* in 1924. Though three of the stories ("A Guilty Woman," "The Dove Came Down," and "The Whistling Swan") were published separately in 1928, internal evidence in *Good-Bye Wisconsin* (31) indicates that the latest work in the collection is the title essay, which was originally published in 1927 in the Sunday book section of the New York *Herald Tribune*. Three of the stories ("Adolescence," "The Sailor," and "The Wedding March") were first published in the collection. Of these three, "Adolescence" is probably the earliest, for it deals with pre-Dan Strane material and could conceivably have been written before 1924. However, technically, the story is much more sophisticated than most of *The Apple of the Eye* and was probably written at the same time as "In a Thicket" or after. From internal evidence, "The Sailor" must have been written after 1925, or after Wescott settled in Villefranche. And "The Wedding March" is too advanced technically to have been written much earlier than 1926. The collection, then, represents work done between 1924 and 1927—mostly, I think, between 1925 and 1927 during the first two years of Wescott's expatriation.

Though all of the stories are set in Wisconsin and are bound to the region by virtue of the details of the physical scene, only a few are regional in the usual sense of the word; most of them could have taken place anywhere in the Midwest or in any rural community; and some of them could have occurred anywhere. The specifically regional stories are "The Runaways," "Prohibition," and "The Sailor." These three resemble "Bad Han" because they are regional portraits in which an attempt is made to depict the life of the uneducated farm people, all of whom are treated as representative types of the region. At first glance, "Like a Lover" seems to belong to this group, but the story is so purely symbolic that it can only be called regional by virtue of its setting. All of the other stories deal with a more sophisticated group of people; and I suppose it could be argued that they continue the regional portraits at this level.

"Adolescence" and "In a Thicket," though one is set in the town and the other in the country, are not really regional at all. Both deal with the theme of knowledge and growth, one through the metaphor of childhood as a series of necessary but frustrating masquerades; the other through a carefully worked out symbolism of light and dark. The four remaining stories deal with adults: three of them are more concerned with love than with the region. The fourth ("The Whistling Swan") is also concerned with love but, more than the others, it links love with the region. The protagonist has just returned from Europe and, ironically, given the title of the book, decides to stay in Wisconsin, primarily because of love. So far as I know, this is the only piece Wescott ever wrote in which anyone willingly remains in the region.

What one is left with, then, is a collection of stories that is loosely regional and finally much more interestingly and profitably considered as a sequence of stories than as a series of regional portraits. Wescott says little or nothing about the region that is new in these stories. Whatever else he had to say about Wisconsin and the Midwest which he did not get into *The Apple of the Eye* and *The Grandmothers*, he put into the strange title essay; and then, three years later, in *The Babe's Bed*, he said his last good-byes and never mentioned it again.

It is not possible to take up all of the stories in *Good-bye Wisconsin* in such a way as to do justice to them individually. Except for *The Babe's Bed*, and isolated instances later on, most of which were "aborted" novels, the stories in *Good-Bye Wisconsin* represent Wescott's only endeavors in the short-story form. They indicate, like *Natives of Rock* and *The Grandmothers*, the rapidity with which he was able to master a form when he was so inclined. And they suggest, as does *Natives of Rock,* that once he had mastered the form, he lost interest in it. Only his interest in, or perhaps obsession with, the novel seems to have persisted; after 1945, he relinquished even that.

The stories in *Good-Bye Wisconsin* are characterized by technical diversity and what strikes one as deliberate experiments in a variety of styles, manners, and forms. "The Runaways" and "Prohibition," for example, are straight narratives, written in a deliberately plain style in which regional dialect is occasionally used. There is little attempt to make either of the stories symbolic. "Prohibition" is the first and last attempt Wescott ever made to use regional material humorously. "The Dove Came Down" and "The Wedding March" are obviously experiments with a particular technique—what might be called the Joyce technique as it is seen in *A Portrait of the Artist as a Young Man.* In both stories, as in *The Grandmothers* and in *The Babe's Bed,* a limited third-person point of view is used, and the story evolves out of interaction between the protagonist and the specific limited scene in which he is placed. The story moves forward at three levels: external action and scenic detail; interior monologue, which includes reverie, meditation, and memory sequences; and symbolism. The stories written in this manner have no plot in the technical sense but have little plots, which consist of the limited number of events which take place in the usually short period of elapsed time in the present. Most of the rest of the story consists of interior monologue or, in the technical sense, stream of consciousness.

In "The Wedding March," for example, the action in the present is the wedding of one Hugo Randolph, but the bulk of the story is devoted to his memory of and meditation on his own initiation fifteen years before into the mysteries of sexual passion, which he mistook for love, by an older married woman. The story has a double resolution: truths about love, passion, and sexuality which are stated in concentrated form at the end of Hugo's interior monologue; and the resolution of the action in the present, which is the departure of Hugo and his bride from the church. The relation between the two parts or plots is obvious. As in "The Dove Came Down," the center of the story is not to be found in the characters but in the technique and theme, and here, the truths of love and passion are more important than the technique.

Love, symbolism, and formal experiments are the real centers in this collection of stories. "Adolescence," in spite of the use of masquerades or disguises as a metaphor for youth, is sexually oriented. Philip is, after all, disguised as a girl; he is once mistaken for a girl at the party and clumsily assaulted by another boy; and almost all of his observations at the party are of the awkward but ferocious "love making" going on all about him. Finally, the relationship between the two boys (Carl and Philip) is described as follows: "On the whole, Carl enjoyed in him [Philip] qualities that he would later enjoy in women" (96). "A Guilty Woman" is entirely concerned with love: it is based upon an actual sequence of events, but certainly what interested Wescott was the "crime of passion" committed by the middle-aged, apparently rational, spinster school teacher. Passion enters her life, after thirty-eight years of purity, as a kind of madness; it makes a fool of her, as it does of almost all lovers in Wescott. Her lover is a cruel libertine who uses her to see what an "old maid's love" is like (138). As in so many of Katherine Anne Porter's stories, the woman is finally pushed beyond the point of reason to temporary madness, commits an act of violence—murder and attempted suicide—and then has to suffer the consequences.

"In a Thicket," like "Adolescence," is covertly sexual, for the escaped Negro convict, the symbolic black man of the story, has committed a crime of passion; and the strange meeting between Lily, the symbolic white girl, and the Negro convict, though not overtly sexual, is described in covertly sexual terms. The last detail—a gash in the screen door—seems rather obvious in its symbolic meaning. Passion, sexuality, and love are among the dark mysteries, the darker rhythms, in Wescott; here they belong to the thicket, the darkness, Negro, isolation, enclosure, prison, innocence, and ignorance cluster, or, in the story's terms, the thicket from which Lily will escape as she awakens from the sleep of childhood, driven forward by her passion (mental and bodily) to know what is out in the darkness.

Even "The Sailor," which, like *The Grandmothers*, combines regionalism and expatriation, but reverses the situation by using Wisconsin as the setting in the present and life in Europe as the main subject, is at least as concerned with love as it is with America and Europe. Terrie Riley, the sailor of the story, is the son of Old Riley, the crippled drunk of the previous story "Prohibition." Terrie has finished his hitch in the Navy, which he joined to escape Wisconsin; has returned, briefly; and is trying to tell his brother what it is like in Europe. His stories consist entirely of encounters with women, chiefly whores, in Villefranche; and the main story is about his relation with a prostitute named Zizi and her relation, in turn, with a Lesbian named Minette, and briefly, about the relations between the three of them. The central point of the story is not to criticize (morally or otherwise) the tangled sexual relationships, but to show that no such complexly tangled possibilities (the dark mysteries of the body, the darker rhythms of sexuality, passion, and love) even exist in Wisconsin and that the self has a "kind of thirst" for them which it must quench if it is to grow (303). The point about Wisconsin and, by implication, all of America is, of course, debatable. However, Wescott does make it frequently, here and elsewhere, during this period, and it does suggest why love and its variants (normal and abnormal) are so important in his work and so consistently linked with the regional material.[7]

"Like a Lover," which is certainly the strangest story in the collection, is also the one in which, to the critic's delight, the thematic and technical centers merge. The story is an almost purely symbolic narrative in regional guise. in so far as there is a central vision in these stories, it is to be found here; and in so far as dominant and characteristic technical tendencies emerge from the collection as a whole, they are also to be found here. The vision is of love, and the techniques are those of the natural symbolist. The story is a repeating narrative: the same fatalistic love story is told twice, with the male lover, a middle-aged widower named Hurst, the same in both versions, but with the women different. The first half of the story tells of Hurst's spellbinding, will-paralyzing effect on Alice Murray. For him, she defies and finally deceives her mother, stealing out at night to meet Hurst and, after her mother has caught and whipped her, running away to marry him. She lives with him only five weeks and then returns to her mother because the spell is somehow broken and she is terrified by her sense that Hurst, who is constantly associated with whips and clubs, is going to kill her some night. Seven years pass, during which Hurst has divorced Alice Murray, and then the story begins all over again. This time the woman is a widow named Mrs. Clayburn who, like Alice Murray, is a seamstress. Alice Murray now assumes the role which her mother played and attempts to keep Mrs. Clayburn from marrying Hurst, not out of jealousy, but because she knows that Hurst will kill her. Alice warns Mrs. Clayburn, who recognizes the truth of what Alice tells her but is unable to break the spell Hurst has on her. She marries him, and the story ends with Alice's friend, Mary Clifford, whipping her "lame, white mare" down the road to tell of the third Mrs. Hurst's death. Alice Murray "fainting away," falls "backward on the porch" (218).

The ending of the story has been implied in the first reference to Hurst, for there one is told that he is a widower who has recently come to Hope's Corner from another state. The effect of the repeating narrative is to suggest that it will all happen again because it is one of the eternal rhythms of love. The language used to describe the effect of Hurst on Alice Murray and Mrs. Clayburn is actually the key to the story and to Wescott's idea of love. "Alice had wondered how she could explain [to her mother] that she was helpless . . . paralyzed . . ." (188). Hurst puts her "under a spell" (197), his arms hold her "like a great rope" (194), and the effect of her marriage on her is "a kind of paralysis" (197). After Alice Murray has warned Mrs. Clayburn that to marry Hurst is to go to her own death, and Mrs. Clayburn realizes that this is true, she replies: "But I've got to do as I must. But I've got to do. . . . Can't help it. I can't help it. I wish I could. . . . I am powerless. Paralyzed . . ." (210, 211). Love, as the story attempts to make clear, destroys all theories, renders knowledge useless and the will powerless; it is deeply, essentially irrational, a kind of madness; it is more powerful than any parental authority or, for that matter, any other kind of authority; it is fatalistic, cruel, and leads to self-sacrifice. In this story it is everywhere associated with death, the instruments of death and brutality—whips, clubs, knives, pitchforks, scissors, and axes—with masochism on the part of the women, sadism on the part of Hurst, and, in the title phrase, with "God [who is] like a lover, waiting, stepping out of the hazel-bushes in the dark, opening his arms . . ." (214).

This particular idea of love, including the religious linkages and the love-death association, has a long, noble, albeit sorrow-ful history. It is not regional, and certainly not exclusively American, but Western and Romantic. It is, in fact, the idea of Romantic love as C. S. Lewis, Denis de Rougemont and, more recently, Leslie Fiedler have explained and chronicled it. The simile in which God is likened to a lover and in which, by implication, Hurst, or any lover, is likened to God, and, finally, by implication, in which love is likened to a god, contains the central idea. Later, in *A Calendar of Saints for Unbelievers,* Wescott was to write a whole witty and sophisticated book about the ways in which God is like a lover, in the sense that He affects people in the same way that a lover or love does, putting them under a spell. The similarity between the love for God and the love for man or woman is that both are forms of passion, and passionate love in any form is a kind of madness, the manifesta-tions of which, regardless of the object, are similar and readily interchangeable. Once the spell of passion is upon a person, and the great substrata of irrational motivation have been released, anything—as Wescott shows here and elsewhere—can happen. There is a strange sense of fatality in Wescott's view of love: a sense of having to submit, or being helpless to resist, this demonic force in all of its manifestations. "Like a Lover" is a dark and cruel story, pervaded by a sense of man's helpless and unwilling (unwilled) acquiescence to a force in himself that is always just below the surface waiting to be released, to take over, whip in hand, and to ride man to his frequently unhappy and almost predestined end. One cannot often throw this rider; one usually outlasts him, lets the passion, whatever form it happens to take, run its course, and hopes for the best.

Such a conclusion about the central vision in a group of stories collected under a regional title and prefaced by an essay which is a strong if somewhat illogical farewell attack on that region seems to leave one nowhere. However, this is not really true, for all regional writers—Faulkner and Frost, for example— not only work, as Wescott did, directly from the region in an attempt to characterize and portray it, but also use regional material to embody a highly personal vision that may, in fact, be representative of or represented in regional material but which finally transcends it. Ratliff, for example, in Faulkner's *The Hamlet,* is as much a Knight Errant as he is a Mississippi sewing machine salesman; and Flem—or phlegm—Snopes is his opposite, the evil knight who must be encountered again and again until he is defeated. This work as a whole (including its two sequels) was surely conceived in Christian-chivalric (that is, Western) terms as a combat to the death between good and evil and then translated into the regional materials available to Faulkner. This, I take it, is what happened in Wescott's case, and it is a good example of how a certain body of regional material can first be used as the basis of regional portraits in fictional form, as in "The Runaways" and "Prohibition," and then as the fictional container or body for other, larger themes, as in "Adolescence," "A Guilty Woman," and "In a Thicket," and finally as the specific material which an author uses, because it is available, to embody a central vision, as in "Like a Lover."

III

"Good-Bye Wisconsin" and *The Babe's Bed,* the first an essay that could be called a story, and the second a story that could be called an essay, belong to a group of four pieces Wescott wrote during this period about returns to America and Wisconsin from Europe. The other two are "The Sailor" and "The Whistling Swan." The essay and *The Babe's Bed* have in common with the two stories a concern with America and the Midwest and an attempt to say something about both of these by using a character who has been to Europe and who conducts his examination of America and the Midwest by opposing it to Europe. The results are almost always the same, because America and the Midwest are never really examined: they are attacked and shown always to be lacking—to be places in which it is impossible to satisfy the hungers of the self. Although the most extreme statement of this position is found in the "Good-Bye Wisconsin" essay, it is also present in both "The Sailor" and "The Whistling Swan," again in an extreme form, but transmuted into fiction and not susceptible to the same kind of analysis as the statements in the essay.

The Babe's Bed, which Wescott says is perhaps "not a story at all, but a melancholy fantasy upon western themes" (8), is the exception; it is not finally an attack on America and the Midwest at all, but a brutal deflation of what Wescott calls the "ephemeral western town in himself, in his mind" where the symbolic babe of the "fantasy" is always "weeping, ungratified, bound in its bed, for its own good."[9] In fact, *The Babe's Bed* is the exception to almost everything Wescott wrote during this period; though it continues and brings to an early and tentative state of perfection the techniques first used in *The Grandmothers,* in every other respect it is the opposite of that work, for it discredits all of Alwyn's towers and in the end calls into doubt all of the natural symbol-making tendencies in Wescott's own mind and fiction. Appropriately enough, it is the last complete work of fiction Wescott published—no one but Wescott knows what he actually wrote—for ten years.

"Good-Bye Wisconsin" (1927) and *The Babe's Bed* (1929) stand in a peculiar relation to each other. Both came out of similar circumstances—Wescott's return to Wisconsin for a visit to his family. But the first was written, I believe, in Wisconsin and published serially in the Sunday book section of the New York *Herald Tribune* at the very height of Wescott's popular and critical fame, and then it was reprinted as the title work in the collection of stories. *The Babe's Bed* was written in November, 1929, in Paris, and published privately in a handsome limited edition of three hundred and ninety-three signed copies by Wescott's great good friend and later sister-in-law, Barbara Harrison. The difference between the two is like the difference between a man's public and private selves; and, as is often true, the private self is much better and more honest than the public one.

"Good-Bye Wisconsin" is almost all manner; a particular kind of style has become a pose, almost that of The Dandy or The Poet on a visit to Wisconsin. The essay is full of beautifully turned hyperbolic statements, witty and barbed aphorisms on

Wisconsin, the Midwest, and America, the truth of which a man could not know with any certainty even after half a lifetime of observation and study. The style is that of the *New Republic* reviews (1923) and the *Transatlantic Review* essay (1925), but perfected now so that it is a very precise and effective verbal tool which carves out an unusually large number of quotable phrases and sentences. The essay has no systematic argument to unify it, but is a hodge-podge of highly wrought fragments elicited by Wisconsin, the Midwest, and America and held together by Wescott's arrival at, brief stay in, and departure from the small Wisconsin town where his family lives. The journey is used as the excuse for pontificating upon everything seen, heard, or thought about on that journey. The variety of subjects and topics covered with an air of authority is staggering: poetry and fiction; politics and religion; fraternities and college presidents; American youth and American love life; the movies and their cultural role; the Midwest in general; American morality; the West; the function of the writer at the present time; and a great many others.[10]

The essay ends with Wescott, to his great relief, on his way back to Europe and meditating upon the two new kinds of novels he would like to write, both non-Wisconsin works: one is to be an indoor book "about ideal people under ideal circumstances" (42), and would thus be the opposite of *The Grandmothers;* the other is to be in a style modeled upon European landscapes, and would thus be the opposite of all the regional, Midwestern, and American work Wescott had so far produced.[11] The essay ends with one of Wescott's sad dreams, a pontification about himself: that of writing a book "out of which myself, with my origins and my prejudices and my Wisconsin, will seem to have disappeared" (45). In a way, this is what the whole essay is and why, now, it seems to be all manner, all verbal posing and posturing. The essay is not really about Wescott saying good-bye to Wisconsin, but about one part of Wescott trying to say good-bye, go away, to another part of himself—what he calls "myself," "my origins," "my prejudices." The two parts, and their geographical equivalents, America and Europe, are both real enough; the irresolution between them, Wescott's inability to resolve the split, is certainly reflected in the fantastic amount of shuttling back and forth between America and

Europe, between his family and his own way of living, which he did during all of the 1920's. In one sense, the style of the essay is not a pose at all, but one of Wescott's two principal voices.

Consciously or unconsciously, *The Babe's Bed* is an answer to "Good-Bye Wisconsin." Or, more accurately, when the story begins and for over half of it, the first voice is speaking; part way through it, the other voice, the private one, says, "No, what nonsense!" and the nameless bachelor passes his hand "across his face as if to brush away an optical illusion." For the rest of the story, the other voice speaks. The second thing it says is probably the most significant: "This was the trouble: suddenly he had lost all sense of independent personalities, and recognized only composite categories of souls: all the sensitive, brutal, and tragic men, all women fumbling in the spell of love as best they could, and all the children" (38). What follows in the story is a systematic de-symbolizing process; a long and painful revelation, as it were, of the degree to which the bachelor had made a fantasy out of the brute realities. There are so many specific revelations in the last part of this loaded story that it would not be possible to cover them without quoting most of the last fifteen pages. However, there are two main ones of great significance to Wescott's development as a whole and to this period in particular.

The first of these has to do with the relation between art and reality, and the second has to do with Wescott himself, or, more properly, his fictional disguise in this story. Since this is the last fictional work published during a period of great productivity— the last so-called regional work Wescott ever wrote, and the last complete fiction he was to publish for ten years—whatever he says here about himself as artist, art, and reality assumes extraordinary importance. It is in this story, more than anywhere else, that he says his last good-byes to the 1920's and to the work that he had done during that period. Wescott once said that he thought of his work during the 1920's as being that of a dead writer.[12] In many ways, he is right; and *The Babe's Bed* is about how and why that writer died, only to be reborn later, like the phoenix referred to in the story, out of his own ashes.

The babe's bed referred to in the title has multiple meanings and functions in the story, and attests once more to Wescott's powers as a natural symbolist. Specifically, it is a harness which, at the bachelor's suggestion, is made and used to tie the baby (who is nameless, like all the other characters in the story) into his crib so that he will not hurt himself during his nightly tantrums. The babe likes to be sung to and rocked to sleep; if this is not done, he throws himself against the sides of the crib, screaming all the while, until eventually he injures himself. The object of the harness is to break him of this habit, to discipline him for his own good and others' peace and quiet. The story moves toward and then away from the first time this harness is used. Involved in the story, aside from the bachelor uncle and the baby, are the mother and father of the bachelor, his un-married sister, his sick married sister, who is the mother of the baby, and her husband.

The story, which is narrated from the limited third-person point of view, with the bachelor as the point-of-view character, is only thirty-five pages long; but like all of Wescott's best work, it is a dense, sometimes elliptical story which, as it develops at three levels, begins to echo and reverberate with meanings. The point-of-view character is the involuter; as the story proceeds, he moves into himself and begins to exfoliate meanings. It is his movement of perception which is the central action of the story. The symbols and fantasies which he exfoliates derive from the physical action in the present, all of which has to do with the family and leads to the main event, which is the placing of the babe in his harness one evening at dinner time.

Up to the turning point, which is the family crisis brought on by the baby's screaming in his harness, the bachelor has followed Wescott's characteristic self-infatuated lyric movement, which, as in the last chapter of *The Grandmothers,* is an almost con-tinuous exfoliation of meaning from the involuted self. The bachelor has either seen everything symbolically from the per-spective of himself or converted everything to symbols and mean-ing; he has indulged himself in a series of grotesque fantasies, all having to do with the baby. He has imagined that the baby is his son, that his married sister is either his wife or mistress because she is the mother of the baby, that he is the baby, and that his sister is his mother and his brother-in-law is thus his father. The end result is a gradual detachment from and distor-tion of the realities of the situation and, as one would expect, a terrible confusion about time and the location of the self in time. When the mundane, even trivial crisis at the dinner table comes, the bachelor is deep in the maze of his own creation; and he further distorts and complicates the situation by erupting into an irrational and petulant rage. Just as he is about to lash out at everyone—to direct, that is, at others a confused rage which ought to be self-directed—he catches himself, gets up, and leaves the room. He now begins to realize the "nightmarish" quality of what he has been doing.

It is at this point that he says to himself, "No, what nonsense!" and passes "his hand across his face as if to brush away an optical illusion" (38). After this the whole story turns in another direction: the exfoliation process is arrested and then systematically discredited. All the rest of the story is involution without exfoliation, for the bachelor has suddenly realized exactly what he has been doing, and he now examines the whole process of exfoliating meanings, the relation of the meanings to the brute realities, and himself as an involuter, a maker of fantasies. He comes, gradually, to three kinds of knowledge: about himself, about the nature of reality, and about the relation between art and reality.

He realizes first of all that he is naturally, maybe incurably, a maker of fantasies, infatuated "with himself," destined to live part of his life "in an ephemeral western town in himself, in his mind . . ." (44). And he realizes also, with the same kind of fatality that is seen in Wescott's idea of love, that he "might as well resolve to agree with this busy force which no name suited better than another—time or nature or destiny or god or anonym. Maniacal worker, mad about its art, invisible and uninvited, it went on darkening with wild strokes their lives that were but scattered square inches of its design" (44-45). Like all of Wescott's lovers, the bachelor acquiesces to his destiny, which happens to be the Towers' malady, the very destiny which Alwyn sought to escape in *The Grandmothers*, for the bachelor is soon to "depart again, to his distant ambitions—the necessary infatuation with himself, the frail glamor of the inappropriate rewards, the remorse incessantly attendant upon his faults . . ." (44). Fittingly enough, going back to the idea of love and the central vision in the stories, the bachelor imagines this "force," his "destiny," gazing "at him personally with its amorous eyes . . ." (45).

The bachelor also comes to realize the extent to which his fantasies, though true of himself, are distortions of the realities external to himself. He realizes, in other words, as Wescott says in the dedicatory note, that "the following vague characters are composed of myself rather than copied from others" (8). If this is true, then his art is not a mirror of external reality, not even an image of it, maybe not even a truthful comment upon it; art is fantasies of the self, another form of self-infatuation— which is exactly what the essay "Good-Bye Wisconsin" is. To a scrupulously honest writer, committed to the idea that art ought to convey truth about experience, about the external world, and certainly about something other than the writer himself, this truth is terrible. What the bachelor comes to realize is that truth, particularized in all of its brutal reality and complexity, is what he witnessed at the dinner table and that "no writer could put these humbler griefs in print." He realizes "that the whole of a book or play, leading up to" these events "would not suffice to make their burden clear" (42). In art, he decides, "only could the worst be said; thus only could the lesson, the sentence entirely and accurately characterizing mankind, the summary truth, be expressed" (43).

These, then, are the last good-byes, only temporary, to be sure; and they are not so much to a region, or to a nation, as to a vocation. Appropriately enough, the last word of *The Babe's Bed* is "asleep"; in that work Wescott as a writer of fiction put himself to sleep for nearly ten years. When he woke himself up, it was to write in *The Pilgrim Hawk* the other half of the "truth" he speaks of in the dedicatory note where he says that *The Babe's Bed* "represents but half, though (I believe) a true half, of the truth" (9).

CHAPTER 5

Style and Truth, 1930-1933

I

IN AUGUST and September of 1931, Wescott and three of his good friends—Monroe Wheeler, Barbara Harrison, and George Platt Lynes—took an automobile trip through Germany. On October 15, 1931, Wescott began what was to be an essay on that tour. Less than five months later—March 3, 1932—he completed the three-hundred and seventy-page book of essays which he entitled *Fear and Trembling*. Like *The Apple of the Eye*, which was first conceived as the story "Bad Han" and then extended into a novel, and like *The Grandmothers*, which was first conceived as a family history, then as a personal memoir, and finally became a novel,[1] *Fear and Trembling* was begun as an essay and ended up as something else.

At some point in the writing of the original essay, Wescott either discovered or decided that he had extremely important things to say which could not be contained in a single essay. He decided to write a collection of essays which would sound a warning to all people who were then concerned about the condition of the Western world. He had given up on the utopian novel—"The Dream of Mrs. Cleveland"—he had been struggling with since 1928 because he thought that "it could serve no purpose in the world of 1931 but that of a soporific."[2] *Fear and Trembling* was to be the opposite kind of work: an extremely serious truth-telling book which would convey both specific and summary truths about the present and future condition of "Christendom" and of mankind in general.

For the reception and success of *Fear and Trembling*, Wescott had the greatest expectations—the hope of the Towers, one might almost say—and the critical and public reception of the book was one of the bitterest disappointments in his writing career. There were few reviews, and almost all of them were extremely harsh. Only *A Calendar of Saints for Unbelievers,* his next book, was received and reviewed more severely. *Fear and Trembling* sold only about nine hundred copies and was eventually pulped by Harper's, which, as Wescott points out with understandable bitterness, is very unusual. Even now, more than thirty years later, Wescott does not like to speak of the book, is reluctant to have anything from it reprinted, and says, "I bitterly regret the way it is written."[3]

Only four years before, in 1927 and 1928, Wescott had been one of the golden boys of American letters. *The Grandmothers,* for example, was a Harper's Prize novel and had an extraordinary popular and critical success. It went through at least sixteen printings between July and August of 1927. *The Apple of the Eye* was well received in 1924 and 1925; two of Wescott's stories—"In a Thicket" and "The Runaways"—were included in the *Best Stories* collections of 1924 and 1925; he had spoken out in the widely circulated New York *Herald Tribune* Sunday book section on American and Midwestern themes; and finally, both in New York and Paris he was directly involved in the literary and cultural life of the times and was a writer one mentioned having seen or met.[4] He had produced so much that was so good while so young that many people regarded him as something of a prodigy: his sudden silence after *Good-Bye Wisconsin* was a cause for wonder and speculation among the critics.

After the initial response to *Fear and Trembling,* there was no other; and Wescott was left in the cruel and absurd position of having made a mighty effort to speak the truth directly in a series of oracular and prophetic essays only to discover that few people wanted to listen. Wescott had written the book in fear and trembling on the assumption that, if something were not done immediately, Western civilization—Christendom, as he calls it—would destroy itself, probably in another Great War. The intensity of Wescott's feelings, his almost maniacal sense of urgency, is indicated by the speed with which he wrote the book, the length of it, and the omnibus nature of the subjects and ideas discussed in it. The book is ejaculatory; it is as if Wescott attempted to express every single truth about reality he ever knew or had thought he knew. The effect created is of a man made heady with his own sudden sense of knowledge; he reels through three-hundred and seventy pages dispensing "truths" with the prodigality of a drunk who thinks his pockets are filled with gold.

No man, drunk or sober, has this many truths to hand out; and, if he proceeds on the mistaken assumption that he does, and in print, the results are liable to be disastrous. After thirty years, Wescott shows uncommonly good sense in bitterly regretting the way the book is written, for where truth *and* style fail together, as they most often do in *Fear and Trembling*, little remains for a later reader but an unintentionally fatuous first-person plural speaker who no longer has much to say, and a very long book which is seldom redeemed by grace or enchantment.

Wescott's other work of this period, *A Calendar of Saints for Unbelievers* (1932),[5] was also written very quickly (in six weeks, Wescott says) and is, like *Fear and Trembling*, a prose work and was, like the other work, a miserable failure, though certainly not a bitter one, for Wescott could not have had the same kind of expectations for its critical or popular success. Though he has never said so, *A Calendar of Saints for Unbelievers* was probably—one wants to say surely—written to relieve the intense, truth-saying ordeal of *Fear and Trembling* and, in some strange way, to compensate for the failure of that book. In spite of the speed with which it was written, no urgency attaches to its composition, and it has no immediate relevance to the times or the terrible problems Wescott attempted to solve in *Fear and Trembling*. Though the theme—variations on the "Like a Lover" idea—is serious enough, the book is almost all style; or, more accurately, the occasion for exercises in a particular, highly sophisticated, and, finally, very limited style. *A Calendar of Saints for Unbelievers* is an act of self-indulgence and the only frivolous book Wescott ever wrote.

The end result of the book is a nadir, a creative dead end which is almost the exact opposite of the point from which Wescott had started nine years earlier with *The Apple of the Eye*. In that novel he had examined the life of a regional saint to discover the truth which it contained; he had applied that truth to his own life and the lives of others victimized by the region and its prevailing Puritan code. The truths had enabled him to escape the region and to set out in search of the bitter apples of experience—the food which the self needed to grow and develop in its own way. But in *A Calendar of Saints for Unbelievers* he makes a stylistic game out of the long-dead saints and their legends; the object is not truth, but witty and sophisticated chronicles of the many Christians who were God's fools. The effect of the style is to raise the chronicler above and to detach him from the subjects whose chronicle he is writing. The book strikes one now as the work of a dilettante who is amusing himself and means to amuse his readers. It is the work of a self no longer in search of truth but settled into a kind of self-satisfied urbanity where the sheer play of the mind is all that is wanted. In this sense the book is frivolous and a prime example of talent wasted and of gifts dissipated.

Because of these points, and at least five others, *A Calendar of Saints for Unbelievers* has a special significance in Wescott's development way out of proportion to its intrinsic worth. It is the last book Wescott wrote in Europe; it is the one exclusively European book he wrote; it is the last book he published before returning to America; it is the last in a series of seven books which he wrote during the extraordinarily productive nine-year period from 1924 to 1933; and it is the last book he published before entering upon the seven years (1933-40) of nearly total silence which he finally broke with *The Pilgrim Hawk*. The two books under discussion here are Wescott's major—almost only—works of the 1930's: both come early in the decade; both are neither fiction nor poetry; and both are, for different reasons, sad failures, examples of a good but restless talent wasting itself, first on a vast project which was beyond its knowledge and power and then upon a frivolous project which was beneath it. Unlike Wescott's fictional and other works of the middle and late 1920's, these two books received the kind of treatment that is cruelest in its effects on an author: they were received first with small derision and then with silence. For an author, even derision is better than silence, for it means that someone, at least, is reading what he wrote: but critical silence is the unanswerable opponent; it leaves the author in a dreadful echo chamber, with the act of communication incomplete and his only reward the sound of his own voice.

The great significance of *The Babe's Bed* is that it is the first overt (though fictional) statement of Wescott's own mistrust of his fiction or of himself as a fiction writer. He apparently came to see his fiction as a deflection from and distortion of reality because of his own tendency toward abstraction and symbol making, and these two processes as forms of self-infatuation. He therefore undertook the opposite kind of endeavor in *Fear and Trembling*, only to have it rejected and his power to perceive truth and present it in any form called into doubt. Wescott's own belief that the artist must transmit the truths of reality in his work was—and is—so profound that this double attack from within and without must have had a shattering effect.

Understandably, Wescott has never said that this is the reason why he would not publish very much—he apparently wrote a great deal—during the rest of the 1930's; but it is probably one of the main reasons for his seven years of almost total silence. And this gives a particular significance to the last works Wescott did before the first of his two prolonged periods of silence began. No serious attempt should be made to redeem either of these two works in their entirety from the partial oblivion into which they fell almost immediately and in which they have remained ever since. What follows is no brief essay at reclamation, but simply an endeavor to see these two works in the context of Wescott's development as a writer and to do such justice to them as seems appropriate after thirty years.

II

At least two thirds of *Fear and Trembling* is nearly unreadable today, for what Wescott says cannot now (and probably could not in 1932) be taken seriously; and the style in which this part of the book is written is not just dull, but is distressing and finally nerve-wracking. Wescott seems to have set down most of what he had to say in what appear to be, even when they actually are not, sentence fragments. The most characteristic stylistic device is the interminable series or the cataloguing technique which Wescott uses so extensively that the forward movement of the book is often arrested for pages and, it seems, sometimes actually reversed. Though the essays are strung on a journey and there are references throughout to this trip and to the four people who made it, a statistical count would probably show that not more than five per cent of the book is devoted to the details of the journey, though there are occasional very good set-pieces in which Wescott describes what he saw.

Most of the book is best described as petulant, indignant, naïve, and confused idealistic sermonizing on a variety of subjects so vast that a committee of experts could not adequately cope with them. In spite of what Wescott says in the Foreword about his distaste for abstractions and generalizing, and in spite of his insistence throughout that what we need to save us—and Christendom—is less idealism and more concrete truth, a greater sense of reality and the basic fundamental brute realities (illustrated and symbolized throughout by positively obsessive references to sexuality); in spite of this, the book is really the work of a fantastic idealist whose main difficulty seems to be that he cannot accept the crass realities of politics, economics, international relations, the church, and other such motivational forces in the public life. The bulk of the book (most of chapters 1-26 and 38-50) is devoted to these public issues; the rest and best part of it (chapters 27-37 and 51) is devoted mainly to the private issues or to the problems of the writer in the modern world.

On the public issues Wescott is clearly an amateur and frequently a poorly informed one; yet he attempts to speak as a well-informed expert on many of these issues and to present his analyses of causes and his solutions with the voice of authority. Much of the book reads like an account of heated bull sessions in which all four of the participants have an opinion on everything. Occasionally these opinions are worth paying attention to because one of the participants hits upon a subject about which he either knows something or about which he can make inspired intuitive statements. But, more often than not, the opinions are merely those of bright, expert talkers who are ready to take up any subject upon almost any occasion and to deliver an opinion on it. Almost without exception, the discussions of economics, politics (especially democracy), international diplomacy, God, religion, the church, Modern Man, and Modern Woman are of the bull-session variety—heated but not very well lighted. It is while reading these discussions that the mind of the reader tends to let go, for it is all talk, talk, talk, and not very good talk at that.

For this reason it seems not only unnecessary but unjust to attempt any kind of systematic treatment of what Wescott has to say on these subjects. These sections of the books are occasionally enlivened, however, by what, thirty years later, have turned out to be prophetic pronouncements on Wescott's part, and it seems only fair to mention that Wescott's reading of the signs of 1931 was not all wrong or all just talk. He saw, for example, with great clarity that Russia and communism were going to emerge as the dominant force to oppose the West in a vast power struggle. He also saw, with the same clarity, that birth control was to become one of the great moral issues of our time; almost everything he says on this subject is relevant today. He also saw that another Great War was simply a matter of time, and that it would be more terrible, more brutal than the first and use instruments of destruction that made those used in World War I seem like children's toys. And he saw, finally—as Joyce, Yeats, Lawrence and many other writers of his time had seen— that one of the central issues of our time was to be the separation of the public from the private life, the separation of the artist from his audience, and, in general, the many conflicts which arise when the demands of the individual private self come to be seen as opposed to the pressure which public life puts upon us and to the values which society upholds.

This and what he has to say about reality and the problems of the writer are actually the overriding themes of the book and the things which are relevant to the reader of *Fear and Trembling* today. About these matters Wescott has a good deal of first-hand knowledge; and, when he writes on these subjects, as he frequently has, he is always worth listening to. In spite of all his protestations and doubts, one of Wescott's great subjects has always been his own private life and his attempts to find reality (truth) and to live in peace and harmony with it, satisfying as best he could the demands of his individual self. In *Fear and Trembling*, for example, it gradually becomes clear that for the speaker and his friends (as for so many other moderns) the old certainties and truths are either gone or discredited, and the problem is how and where to find new ones that will give direction and meaning to their lives. The solution offered is actually a very simple one: the truths of reality must become the new God; man's salvation lies in his being able to discover as many of these truths as possible and then learning how to live with them. By truths of reality Wescott does not mean abstract truths; he means the basic, even brute realities of man's nature and of the world in which he lives. Food (the market in Paris—Les Halles—is one of the main symbols of reality in the book), drink, health, sickness, sexuality, sensuality, death, sorrow, unrequited love—these are some of the realities and truths. Most of the truths in the book are like this; they are the basic realities of everyday living, the recurrent experiences of the private life.

The book ends with a parable, a simple, forceful tale told by someone of Tolstoi, who "stopped a man ploughing in a field, and asked him what he would do if he knew that the world was coming to an end the next day." After thinking a bit, the peasant answered, "I would plough" (369). And this is the whole point of the book, really: the ploughing is the truth, the reality, the need and necessity, the routine act of the daily life. Comparable things could be found in any man's life, and a certain number of universal recurrent things can be found in all men's lives. This is the god one must worship, whose commands one must obey, whose truth one must disseminate. The man ploughing is comparable to the baby crying in *The Babe's Bed;* and all idealisms, all theories, are similar to the narrator in that story who cannot hear or see the baby for the symbols and who finally devises the harness so that an abstract principle of discipline may be carried out. Of such mundane truths as the fight at the dinner table in *The Babe's Bed* is reality composed: these are greater than any fiction, more powerful and moving than any theory, more important to experience and knowledge than any system or idea.

Though *Fear and Trembling* is a public document in the sense that it is deliberately addressed to and needs an audience, its message is that the public ills which plague the modern world could best be cured by less preaching and sermonizing, by less peddling of ideals in the market place, and by more living in accordance with the nature and demands of the self and reality. The solution to the public problem is to perfect (in the sense of living fully) the private life of the self. As countless other modern writers have shown, this is no simple-minded solution to a complex problem; actually, it is a common modern solution to an acute modern problem on both sides of the Atlantic.

Writers as different as E. B. White and Katherine Anne Porter, E. M. Forster and James Joyce, D. H. Lawrence and Henry Miller have spoken out with Wescott on this issue, though, in and out of their works, each has gone about it in different ways because each, as one might expect, has discovered different realities—different truths in accordance with which the self perfects its private life.

Wescott speaks so often on these points—the self, reality, and the private life—in *Fear and Trembling* that at best one can only give a sample of what he says. The problem, as so many writers have understood it since the late nineteenth century, is in part one of perception:[6] "the modern eye," Wescott says, "has been trained, not to see things, but to see through them . . ." (227). Man, Wescott says, has always had a "tendency to cringe, and to dream in ideal terms, and to look down upon little radical facts"[7] (237). "Moral imagination as the truth's constant antagonist, or as a means of flight from experience, is one of the fatal faculties . . ." (238). The moral imagination, dreaming in ideal terms, then, is a way of not seeing the basic realities, the "little radical facts." This leads to what Wescott calls "the old secretiveness," a kind of blindness to reality: "so long as the old secretiveness lasts, so long as we are expected positively not to face the facts of what we all do and, in spirit and flesh, all that privately happens, how," he asks, "can we learn to face and quietly deal with the new state of affairs?" (255). "If we are to do anything at all," he insists, "beyond these adventures in mathematics, chemistry, surgery, physics, etc., if we are to last long enough to have been anything, among history's various masterpieces, it must be by admitting, learning from, imagining— well, the plain truth. The whole plain truth: evidently there is, can be, no other God for us, not in any case until that one has got His work done" (258).

"The miracle called for now," according to Wescott, "is in the nature of a descent upon our earth of the coldest truths, the humblest virtues . . ."[8] (265). This would be the descent of the new God upon earth; for, as Wescott says later in the book, "God is the truth, the whole truth (including the plain truth), what was and is and will be" (326). This is what Wescott thinks will save us, and to point this out is surely the chief reason he wrote *Fear and Trembling*, which not only affirms this point over and over again, but contains many of what Wescott takes to be these "cold," "plain," "whole" truths and "humblest" virtues. Wescott says, for example, that "human business is—not to try to dream the whole—but to be the part, to be, to be absorbed in the being, right to the end" (335). This is the central point in the defense of the private life of the self, in the living of life. The great enemy—what keeps men from going about their business—is Gatsby's disease: "the most dangerous of fictions (one decides finally) is that of the ideal, the ideal God, God-beside-the-point . . ." (340). "To be, to be absorbed in the being" is to know that "eating and digesting and falling in love and begetting other beings and increasing other things are as divine as God" (345). Coming around again to the central point of the book—and really the central point Wescott first made in *The Apple of the Eye* and has continued to make ever since—he says of the divinity of the basic realities: "we must really feel it, and act accordingly—or we are lost, done, done for" (345).

And he really does mean it. The way to destruction, he says, individually and collectively, is to pile up fictions in our minds. By fictions he means the whole fiction-making process whereby untruths are invented—and all ideals, all theories, all abstractions —from experience.[9] In an apparent paradox, Wescott argues that reality is the one true source for fiction, and in this way comes round to what he calls the task of the artist in the modern world. Early in the book, Wescott had asked how anyone had the "courage to make up mysteries, to invent plots, while the master of all the forms of fiction (one might as well call him God) is still at work?" (62-63). Later he answers this question by equating truth with God and by arguing at length that the task of the artist these days is "truth-telling" (216). Not "provocation, but instruction and a general sense of radiance and shapeliness are what fiction has to give" (169). According to Wescott, the artist must be either a realist or nothing these days, and his truths (of the cold, plain, whole variety mentioned above) must be of two kinds—both of which, interestingly enough, can be illustrated by the only other two pieces of sustained fiction Wescott ever published.[10]

The first kind of truth which the artist can use as the basis of fiction can be called the truths of the author's own private experience. In writing about this subject, the author gives "himself as an illustration, an example of destiny in his day." Though he can write a true factual account, usually the artist presents these truths in "some sort of transparent fiction" or some kind of "symbolical fiction" (223). The second kind of truth which the author can aim at is accurately to "mirror" his own "day and age" or "the look of life" in his own time, "so that the busier healthier commoner man could find in writing, in focus, what he was doing, and thus be helped to grasp its meaning, and, by reactions of shame and enthusiasm before the conveniently concentrated picture, be led to take himself and all the rest somewhat more seriously than before" (220-21).

With these points about the task of the artist in the modern world the discussion of *Fear and Trembling* may be brought to its almost necessarily ironic conclusion. The first kind of truth and the transparent or symbolical fiction have always been what Wescott naturally tended toward. His destiny was to use himself as an example of destiny in his own day. And yet, from the early 1930's on, it has been the second kind of truth and fiction which Wescott has set up as his own ideal. Failing to attain this ideal he has, over the years, seemed more and more to become a victim of his own towering conception of the artist and of the kind of novel he feels should be written.

III

Though *A Calendar of Saints for Unbelievers* strikes one as a frivolous and self-indulgent book, it is not all this way and was probably not meant to be taken so lightly. The whole book consists of variations upon a quotation from *Fear and Trembling* to the effect that "the most dangerous of fictions . . . is the ideal, the ideal God, God-beside-the-point." With a few exceptions, the saints whose lives Wescott chronicles are examples of people who failed "to be, to be absorbed in the being." They are people who died for God, or, more exactly, denied the world for love of God. Most of the saints were victims of two fanatical idealisms: their own and that of their enemies. Because of either or both of these idealisms, the saints were frequently boiled, flayed, quartered, or otherwise done away with. Some of the saints were not tortured to death, but they themselves mortified the flesh in extreme and certainly barbarous ways, all for the love of

God. The Rose of Lima entry for 30 August is characteristic: "This South American saint was an exceedingly pretty seam-stress. Holy at heart as she was, her beauty embarrassed her. When she had to wear roses in her hair, she fixed them so that they made a crown of thorns for herself, however they may have looked to others. Finally she burned her face away, with applications of quicklime" (131).

This last brutality of detail is repeated over and over again in the book, along with acts of sadism and masochism, stupidities, follies, various perversions and aberrations all of which, in another context, have been and still are held up as pious and saintly exemplars of the triumph of the spirit over the flesh, of God over everything else. A few of the saints (Joan of Arc and Saint Francis, for example) Wescott seems genuinely to admire and to hold up, as he did Bad Han, as authentic saints from whom one can learn something about living in the world. Those whom he admires are without exception people of action who devoted themselves primarily to the practical problems of this world.

If any lessons are to be derived from the majority of the entries, they are mostly negative ones: for an unbeliever, these are not people who died or were killed for God, but people who were victims of love. In this context, the saints become fools of love and examples of a negative truth: all of them gave up the world, the realities, for an abstraction, an idealism. They illustrate a point Wescott makes in his Foreword: "Perhaps love is always sexual. And it is usually hopeless, sooner or later; ignorant, from first to last; thankless, too soon" (ix). The saints, then, are examples of what not to do, of a destiny which, if possible, one should try to avoid. It is in this sense that they are saints for unbelievers—those who cannot or will not accept "the creed and its corollaries" (viii)—because, once detached from the church and God, for whom they sacrificed themselves or were sacrificed, the saints all become pitiable victims of Wescott's rapacious, blind, and cruel god of love.

This view of love is one of the principal truths which Wescott feels he has discovered and should convey to the public. It is certainly not frivolous, and Wescott usually treats it, in the manner of Racine in *Phaedra,* as a hopeless, violent, destructive passion which reason can recognize but is helpless to combat. *A Calendar of Saints for Unbelievers,* however, is an extremely witty, ironic, and sophisticated treatment of this subject. To compile a calendar of saints, all of them Christian, for un-believers is, to begin with, to make a book based on an under-lying irony. Every entry contains an implicit irony, for horror is piled on horror and set against a covert expletive: See what has been done in the name of God! But no serious, systematic attack is ever mounted against God or the church, and the cumulative force of the examples is constantly dissipated by various forms of wit, principally understatement, and devices of style which make it difficult to take the whole seriously. The resulting tone, which is established in the Foreword, is light and sophisticated as one characteristic passage illustrates perfectly:

> Here and there, obviously, I have spoken for myself, spoken out—hissed or mumbled my platitudes of the time being. I could not help it. They should not be taken too seriously; doubtless they will not be taken seriously enough. It is a matter of emotion rather than of deliberate opinion. Chameleon emotion, the sincerest thing on earth; real tears shed in the action of this revived play of faith; giggles at a funeral—and it may be my own funeral (vii).

At every point in this passage where a serious point is about to be made, Wescott cancels it by a variety of stylistic tricks and effects. For example, "hissed or mumbled" to describe the way in which truths are delivered; the coy qualification—"not too seriously"—of how his truths should be received; the punning phrase "revived play of faith" to describe his use of the saints; the unfortunate use of the word "giggles," in fact the whole un-fortunate image; and finally, the extremely clever last phrase, so witty it could not possibly be taken seriously following hard upon the "giggles at a funeral."

Wescott also says in the Foreword that he does "not care to write untruths. . . ." and that *A Calendar of Saints for Un-believers* contains two kinds of truth: historical truth, or "the thing that happened"; and truths of the self, or "the thing that did not happen, which is none the less true of thought or feel-ing . . ." (viii). The distinction Wescott is making is between recorded history—what was done and said, even some of the reasons for these things—and unrecorded history—what was thought and felt, why certain things were done and how they affected the people who did them and to whom they were done. That *A Calendar of Saints for Unbelievers* contains both kinds of truth is not being questioned; what is wrong with the book is the attitude taken toward the truths (and the reader) and the style Wescott used to present them. The attitude is one of pleasant intellectual indulgence (toward the material and the reader), and the style (which establishes and sustains the attitude) is playful, coy, sometimes giggly, and generally without distinction or power. It is an easy style; in fact, the whole book is an "easy" endeavor; and this is precisely what is wrong. It seems like a waste of time and, given Wescott and the nature of the material, a terrible waste of energy and talent.

Unlike *Fear and Trembling*, this book has none of the heat and passionate (if misguided) intensity of serious discussion; it is like an after-dinner conversation, very urbane and somewhat effete. Though it was probably not meant to be so, *A Calendar of Saints for Unbelievers*, when considered in relation to Wescott and the times, is a very sad book: it is a testament of his failure and a great falling off from the achievements of the 1920's and the towering intentions of *Fear and Trembling*. A retreat into style, urbanity, and effeteness on the part of a dedicated and committed man is always sad to witness. To be sure, this tendency was always present in Wescott:[11] but to have left Wisconsin and one's native land, to have gone east and eventually to Europe in search of what America lacked in order that the self might be fulfilled and art created, and to have produced something like *A Calendar of Saints for Unbelievers* as the end-work of this eastern movement is, in Fitzgerald's phrase, to have dissipated one's resources, to have made "nothing out of something."

The Apple of the Eye, in spite of its faults, is a much better book than *A Calendar of Saints for Unbelievers* because it aims at more and has more truth in it—of style as well as content. The failures in *The Apple of the Eye* are not the result of a deliberately contrived intention but of inexperience and lack of knowledge. Where Wescott succeeds in that book—as in the "Bad Han" and "Dan Alone" sections—he is very good, and those portions are so much better than anything in *A Calendar of Saints for Unbelievers* that it makes the nine years which elapsed between the two books seem like a regression. Wescott mastered a variety of styles, to be sure, and in a sense the tools of his vocation; but he either misused that mastery or wasted it on a trivial project. It is in this sense that *A Calendar of Saints for Unbelievers* represents the extreme counter-movement away from Wescott's origins and true creative sources. This one failure does not mean that he could not write about Europe, for he did so brilliantly in *The Pilgrim Hawk*; it means that neither in subject nor in style does *A Calendar of Saints for Unbelievers* approximate what Wescott thinks art should be or what he is capable of doing well. Wescott's best source of truth has always been himself, his private and somewhat peculiar movements of self; he has seldom written well on any other subject. To deny this fact, as he has often done, and to attempt other things has almost always proved disastrous.

A *Calendar of Saints for Unbelievers* is such a disaster; and more than that, actually, it is a dead end. Without a style that is in any way compelling or enchanting, which lacks, in Edmund Wilson's phrase, any kind of "personal radiance," and without many truths to compel an assent to the author's vision, the book represents the artist become dilettante—the artist deflected in an extreme way from what Wescott takes to be his true high purpose. If Wescott bitterly regrets the manner in which *Fear and Trembling* is written, he should also bitterly regret everything about *A Calendar of Saints for Unbelievers;* for in many ways it is an example of what, way back in the early 1920's, he attacked as a debasement of art and the artist. If this is all that eight years in Europe could produce, then Wescott certainly did the right thing when, almost immediately after the publication of this book, he returned to America for good. And it is certainly significant that he never again attempted (or published) anything remotely similar to this book.

He could not go on in the direction of the *Calendar;* he could not go back to the regional material; he did not wish to or could not go back to poetry; and his oracular and prophetic book of essays had been rejected by the public and critics. He had apparently exhausted Europe, just as he had, in his own mind, exhausted certain bodies of material, certain forms, and certain techniques. He was not necessarily at either a dead end or a nadir, but he was surely at a still point where reassessment was necessary before it would be possible for him to move out in a new direction or farther forward to some point beyond what he had achieved earlier. The period of great creativity began with the movement which culminated in Wescott's prolonged expatriation; it ended with the termination of the expatriation and the reversal of the movement. In 1933 Wescott came home.

CHAPTER 6

The Abortive Years, 1933-1939

I

WHEN WESCOTT returned to America, he settled first in
New York City, where he shared an apartment with his
brother, Monroe Wheeler, and George Platt Lynes. In 1943 he
moved to the family enclave in New Jersey, where he has lived
ever since. This return to America brought to a close the twelve
years of restlessness and travel which had begun in 1921; it
signified the end of Wescott's eight years of expatriation; and it
marked the end of his deliberate separation from his family,
which had begun at least as early as 1918. During the 1930's,
Wescott twice returned to Europe; first in 1935 to accompany
his brother and new sister-in-law, Barbara Harrison, and again
in 1938 for what he called inspirational reasons. He was to go
again to Europe later, but since 1933 Wescott has, so far as I
know, mostly stayed at home.[1]

The six years between 1933 and 1939 are best understood, I
think, as the time in which Wescott waited out the first of his
two long, unproductive periods. These are the abortive years:
during this time Wescott lost at least three (and probably more)
of his fictional children and apparently was unable either to
stop trying or to stop aborting. His development now takes on
an entirely different character; just as suddenly as he had come
upon the literary scene and contributed extensively to it, he
withdrew from it and stopped contributing almost completely.
In seven years he published only three stories, "Hurt Feelings"
in 1932, "The Rescuer" and "The Sight of a Dead Body" in
1936; two essays, "A Sentimental Contribution" in 1933 and
"Praise" in 1939[2]; and one poem, "Summer Ending" in 1939.

Oddly enough, the published work of these seven years is
uniformly good, and some of it is exceptional. "Summer End-

ing," for example, is one of the best poems Wescott ever wrote; the two essays, which belong to a sizable group of lyric essays Wescott has written since the late 1920's, are both fine works (the one on Katherine Anne Porter is among the best pieces ever written about her fiction); "Hurt Feelings" has sections in it which are extremely good, and "The Sight of a Dead Body," though brief, is a precise, carefully wrought episode.

This period in Wescott's career, like the one from 1945 to the present, poses interesting and perhaps insoluble problems; for what he did not publish looms much larger than what he did. As in the mysterious case of E. M. Forster, when a good and previously prolific writer suddenly stops creating, one has a situation which is almost irresistibly fascinating; the temptation is to speculate, often wildly and usually along psychoanalytic lines, about the reasons for the sudden cessation. One assumes that the artist should keep on creating, more or less regularly, and develop, more or less steadily, both his craft and his vision. Because of the public nature of his endeavor, the artist in stasis is a man who has probably unwillingly exposed his private difficulties to public scrutiny. His inability or unwillingness to produce what is expected of him is immediately interpreted as a failure of talent or will, rather than, say, as a period of readjustment and reassessment. The reasons for so sudden a cessation as Wescott's must always be enormously complicated, essentially private, and ultimately inaccessible unless the private papers of the artist are available for study.[3]

In Wescott's case, as in those of Fitzgerald and Forster, one can say with certainty that there was no question of his having exhausted what talent he had, in abundance, from the beginning; and no question, really, as some critics have argued, of his having depleted the regional material and not being able to find any other. These explanations are too simple; so is one of Wescott's own: the specious proposition that what happened to him in the 1930's is that, given the times, "it was down with Wescott and up with Farrell. . . ."[4] All of the internal evidence— most notably *The Babe's Bed* and its sequel, *The Pilgrim Hawk,* the two works that bracket this period—suggests that a passion for reality and a growing distrust of his own ability to convert truth to fiction in a narrative form that was adequate and yet did not distort the truth are among the primary reasons why

Wescott partially silenced himself then and later as a writer of fiction. Other evidence, such as Wescott's idea of the novel and his sense of what the function of the artist *must* be—both of which he presents in detail in *Images of Truth* and in miscellaneous essays written from the late twenties on—suggests also that no outside forces, no set of historical, political, and economic conditions, stunned him into silence, but that he silenced his fiction-making self because he did not want to be a purveyor of lies. Even though the 1930's are filled mostly with silence, these years are actually a crucial period: the three stories represent a dying fictional voice; and the essays, especially the one about Henry James, are the new voice, a small one to be sure, but one that was to persist for the next thirty years.

II

The three fictional works which Wescott released for publication during the 1930's do not require very extensive discussion, for all seem to be fragments of longer works and one is so clearly a rescued episode that to evaluate it as a completed work would be unjust. The three "stories" are chiefly interesting as the remains of the type of fiction that Wescott attempted to write during the abortive years. They are examples, in a strange way, of failures, not necessarily in their own right, but because Wescott would not or could not carry them to completion. The first, longest, and most complete of these is "Hurt Feelings," published in 1932 in the *North American Review*. Though it is not clear to what extent "Hurt Feelings" is a rewriting and condensation of material from "The Dream of Mrs. Cleveland," the fact remains that it is all that was ever published of the "utopian" novel Wescott had described in the essay "Good-Bye Wisconsin" (42-43) and had begun to write around 1928. He abandoned it in 1931 because he thought it had nothing important to say at that time. The story, then, has a special significance because it is all that remains of Wescott's first fictional abortion and because the abandoned novel was the first piece of sustained nonregional fiction Wescott had tried to write.

When the story opens, John Durn is slowly but painlessly dying from old age. Only his "will" or "soul" keeps him alive, and he will remain so only as long as, within the predatory bird metaphors used throughout, there is still some body left for him to feed upon. In the first section of the story, one learns that John Durn was one of the self-made, fabulously wealthy American capitalists of the nineteenth century. The scene shifts from his bedroom to his den, where his daughter, Mrs. Cleveland, is going through his private papers. There she discovers the secret of his life and the key to the knowledge that saves her. The secret is the love "hurt" which John Durn received, inadvertently, from his wife when, early in their marriage and in his career, she had said that Durn's partner Joseph Gilson was, in some respects, a better man and businessman. These are the hurt feelings of the title; they lead to a jealous rage in the soul of John Durn that is so great he spends the rest of his life taking his revenge on his wife, Joseph Gilson, his daughter, his son-in-law, and even his grandson. The triple irony here is that this deflection of love is the real source of Durn's financial success; that this rage in the soul slowly consumed him; and that, contrary to popular opinion, there is nothing great about him save the size of his fortune. Sections three and four of the story are a condensed chronicle of the origin and development of his rage and its consequences.

In section five the story returns to Mrs. Cleveland, still going through the private papers and about to begin the long coming-to-knowledge which continues to the end. Now, Joseph Gilson, the ex-partner whom Durn has systematically ruined again and again by stealth, double dealing, and legal frauds, hears that Durn is dying and comes to pay his last respects. The last four sections have an alternating structure: Gilson, ignorant of the fact that Durn has caused all of his failures, keeps trying to make clear to Mrs. Cleveland just why Durn was a great man: at the same time Mrs. Cleveland has her sequence of revelations in which she realizes that her father is not a great man, that he is really a kind of monster who has thrown away his life for an idea and who has nearly succeeded in ruining her life, as well as that of her son and husband. She decides that it is Gilson and her husband—the saints, fools, and failures who want only to live—who are the great men. As the story ends, Mrs. Cleveland is only waiting for her father to die so that she may use her knowledge to save her son from "morbid greatness" and perhaps even effect a reconciliation between herself and her husband, whom the father had long ago recognized as a threatening rival and had sent away with a life-long gratuity.

The story, as can be seen from this descriptive summary, is basically a long self-revelation which ends with a familiar Wescott truth. Like Alwyn Tower, Mrs. Cleveland is less a character than a perceiver and realizer of this truth—someone who can move through the pattern, come to the truth, and act upon it. She resembles most of the other central characters in Wescott's fictions, and her movement of perception gives the story its basic structure (the plot is incidental) and is the characteristic movement toward reality and truth found in all of Wescott's works. Thus, the story is like many of the stories in *Good-Bye Wisconsin* in technique; resembles all of his fictional works in its characteristic movement; has the same specific theme as *The Babe's Bed, Fear and Trembling,* and *A Calendar of Saints for Unbelievers;* and works with the same subjects—love, death, and truth—that have absorbed Wescott from the beginning.

The two new things are the use of non-regional material and the extent to which the story is apparently a contrived fiction. These two things represent attempts by Wescott to get away from himself and the immediate details of his own life as the sources of his fiction. In this respect, the story is quite different from much of the earlier work, even though some of the stories in *Good-Bye Wisconsin* are also attempts at the same things. Wescott tried again in "The Rescuer" to write what can be called an "outside" narrative; and, still later, he attempted and finally succeeded in writing a whole novel—*Apartment in Athens* —in this manner. "Hurt Feelings," then, is one of the first and fairly successful attempts he made to produce fiction in which he was not the central character or intelligence.

"The Rescuer" (1936) is almost unique among Wescott's published work; it is the only incoherent piece (story or essay) which he ever released. It is like "Hurt Feelings" in the sense that it clearly represents another attempt to write an "outside" narrative. Given the fact that Wescott has always been a careful, even meticulous worker, and that even his fair-to-poor works have been characterized to an unusual degree by formal unity, the incoherence and the incompleteness of this story are very puzzling. Perhaps the most plausible explanation is that the story is all that remains of a longer work, maybe a novel, and that at this point Wescott was not even willing (or was unable) to salvage a coherent fragment from it, as he had done with "Hurt Feelings." Why he released it for publication is even more mysterious, for Wescott has never made a practice of clearing his files periodically just to get published. Always scrupulously honest with himself, he has not released things which did not meet his own very high standards of truth and excellence. According to Sy Kahn, for example, Wescott has trunks of material which he will not release because he does not think it is good enough.[5]

"The Rescuer," then, remains a question mark which is probably best described briefly and passed by. The story is narrated from an omniscient third-person point of view which shifts about halfway through to a limited third person, with Martin Herz (a journalist) as the focusing character. The story breaks in two and actually falls apart after the shift is made. The first part of the story presents a series of sensational events: four young boys decide to spend the night in an abandoned house in a "far suburb of New York," the house catches fire, a mysterious man drives up, rushes into the house, rescues one of the boys (an identical twin), rushes back into the house and disappears. Three of the boys die in the fire, and the rescued twin dies a few months later, unable to live without his other half. The mysterious rescuer turns out, after many false rumors, to have been a notorious hoodlum, and the abandoned house to have been a secret hangout, opium den, bar, arsenal, hiding place for blackmail evidence, and assorted other things. The rescuer had rushed into the house to save his loot, not the boy, and had performed a spontaneous act of rescue. At this point, Martin Herz is introduced into the story along with a bereaved Sunday school teacher who is guilt-ridden, as she informs Herz, because she had told three of the boys the story of Daniel, Nebuchadnezzar, Shadrach, Meshach, and Abednego, and had insisted that, if the boys had done no evil, they too would be rescued from fire.

The end of the story is all Martin Herz's interior monologue, part of which is devoted to extracting the meaning from the events and part to the sudden introduction of all kinds of complications into the story which are never developed and never resolved. The last paragraph is a jumble of confused symbolic meanings which Wescott attempts to attach to Martin Herz. One cannot decide where or what the center of the story is, for the meaning of the title is complicated by gratuitous remarks all through the last part, and Martin Herz simply does not exist as a character and does not even function successfully as a perceiver and realizer of truths. The story ultimately strikes one as notes or sketches for a longer work, maybe even a novel which Wescott abandoned for unknown reasons. Aside from the fact of its confusion and ultimate failure, "The Rescuer" differs from "Hurt Feelings" in one way which may explain why Wescott abandoned it: half of the story is outside narrative and half of it is inside narrative. Martin Herz is really Alwyn Tower with another name and in this sense is a return to the very things Wescott was trying to get away from in his fiction: the self-infatuations of the bachelor in *The Babe's Bed*, the morbid involutions of the incurably abstracted mind.

The third and final story which Wescott published in the 1930's, "The Sight of a Dead Body" (1936), completes a kind of circular movement which can be traced through these stories; in it Wescott literally returns to his beginnings. The only character in this story is Michael Byron, and he was one of the main characters in *The Apple of the Eye*. The shortest of the three stories, this one is set in New Jersey on a farm and is narrated throughout from the limited third-person point of view. Like the other two stories, it deals in some way with the trio of death, love, and truth. There is a single event, the discovery of the dead body: it is preceded and followed by Michael Byron's perceptions, memories, and reveries. The story is not only very short, but slight: there is not really any systematic symbolism, but only the presentation of this episode in Michael Byron's life. Wescott does not attempt to extract a heavy burden of meaning from the episode, which he certainly could do; he merely presents it, cleanly and objectively.

Unlike "The Rescuer," this story is very satisfying: its power comes from the uniformly good prose and from the sharp and effective contrast between the lush images of the spring scene and the stark brutal images of the naked, faceless, dead body atop the dung heap. The story appears to have been written for the sake of the contrast between these two realities, with Michael Byron functioning primarily as a perceiver of them. Aside from the presence of Michael Byron, the story is a throwback in another sense, for the technique is primarily that of the Imagist poems in *Natives of Rock;* it is without a plot, without characters in conflict, and could easily have been written as a long lyric poem. Such truth as there is in this story is all in the images—and in them as perceived rather than as laboriously interpreted in the manner of Alwyn Tower, Martin Herz, or Mrs. Cleveland.

In some ways, this is the best of the three stories, for Wescott here records with great precision of language the perceived images of external reality and presents them for their own sake as a tribute to the nature of reality itself. Wescott is also able to record, with the same precision and beauty of language, the movements of the self (primarily his own) which constitute an internal reality. His talent has never been for invention, but for observation and interpretation. The significance of the lyric essays which he began to write in the 1930's is that in them he discovered a form which was ideally suited to his talents and needs as a writer: in these essays he was under no compulsion to invent; he had only to record and interpret, often in the most minute detail and as accurately as possible.

The earliest of these essays appeared in 1930 in *The Bookman;* its ostensible subject was Wescott's friend and fellow novelist, Elizabeth Madox Roberts. The key to what Wescott was doing in this and later lyric essays is given in the subtitle, where he calls it a "personal note." As much or more about Wescott as it is about Miss Roberts, the essay presents, in a hypnotic style of long, packed, sensuous sentences, Wescott's total response to Miss Roberts as a person, a friend, a novelist, and a poet. What one discovers in rereading this and other similar essays is that Wescott has completely absorbed Elizabeth Madox Roberts in all the ways that he has known her, that the different things about her have become inseparable, and that she, as a whole, has been so thoroughly taken into himself that he cannot write of her in any other way than personally—in terms of himself, where the external and internal realities have been fused. The result is an essay which has a very complex structure: the center of it is not just Wescott but his multiple experiences of Elizabeth Madox Roberts. In order to present these, Wescott must move in and out of himself, back and forth through time, from place to place where he has known her, from prose to poetry, and from first to later readings of a given work.

Wescott's lyric essays are about himself or about writers he has known in either of two ways: personally as with Elizabeth Madox Roberts, or through their works so profoundly and over so long a period of time that his knowledge of them has become a direct personal experience, as with Henry James. The essay, "A Sentimental Contribution," which Wescott wrote for the *Hound and Horn* Henry James issue (1934) is an almost classic example of a very disciplined, rigorous kind of impressionistic (that is, lyric) criticism, where the writer begins with uncommon honesty by frankly admitting that he is going to consider a given author in terms of his own experience of and response to him. This is half the meaning of the word "sentimental" in the title (the other half will emerge as this discussion proceeds). Wescott begins his essay, for example, with a section entitled "Memory as Criticism" and devotes it to an exact description of how he and one of his sisters—both young, innocent, and living in rural Wisconsin—first read Henry James "seated in a high hard-wheeled three-seated second-hand automobile which wound up noisily on the left side" and "wept" over him (VII, 522). They wept, he says, "probably because life . . . appeared to us to be what he [James] maintained that it was, in his international world, in the romantic distance" (VII, 524). "Mere mortals," Wescott says, "are all inclined to weep when a momentary situation or emotion seems about to go on forever. The whole of life, abroad as at home, so Henry James said, was adolescence; therefore we wept" (VII, 525).

From this rather obscure point—which seems to be that in reading Henry James, whom they believed to be true, they were convinced that the future, at home or abroad, would be just the same as the present; deprived of their bright hopes for a better life ahead, they wept—Wescott moves to his second major point: that though James had no literary influences on him, he did, more than any other writer, influence his "morals" (VII, 525). In James's "middle and late fiction," Wescott says, are to be found his "morals and perhaps the moral" (VII, 526). From James, Wescott derived, he says, an ideal mode of existence—urbane, cultured, civilized—which he tried to achieve in his own life. From his Jamesian-derived morals, Wescott then moves to the moral, for himself and his own generation, which is that "there is no warning in Henry James; his tales are too much in moderation" (VII, 529). What Wescott means is that James either leaves out too many realities or does not deal adequately with them.

In the second section, "A Suggestion to the Studious," Wescott addresses himself to what he thinks writers need to do in 1934: his central point is that what is submerged in James, what is kept in the background and dealt with only by suggestion or in such a way as to form an "underplot," must be brought into the foreground and made the chief subject of the writer. As Wescott correctly points out, many of James's middle and late works "appear to have originated in, and with elegant subterfuge display, excitement about some bold, sad, and scabrous problem, some overt perversity or real bad behavior" (VII, 531). Examples of this are too numerous to mention: what is important here is the point Wescott makes about James, which is that his art is "emotionally equivocal" because "the rich effect of emotion which he produces on almost every page is not really justified by the sense of the work as a whole. Embarrassed passion, hinted meaning, are in excess of the narrated facts; the psychic content is too great for its container of elegantly forged happenings; it all overflows and slops about and is magnificently wasted" (VII, 532-33). This is the central point Wescott has to make about James, and he uses it to set up a sequence of points about the nature and function of art, especially in the modern world.

"Such an emotionally equivocal art does not give as much satisfaction to mature men and women as it does pleasure to adolescents" with their "green intellects" and "untried hearts." "The time comes," Wescott says, "when a merely moral extortion, a merely hypothetical assault, the war of the sexes just in the abstract, and so forth, must fail to stir a hardened, perhaps even scarred personality." He and his sister, for example, would not now weep over Henry James for they "have seen too much worse trouble"; or, if they did weep, he says that "it would be dryly, wryly, abstractly" (VII, 533). Wescott then states what is the central point of the essay—or the central truth—as it has emerged from his experience of James, his own experience as a

writer, his observations of the modern world, and his conclusions about the relation of art to the individual in the modern
world:

> Perhaps the time has come when composite emotions and sug-
> gestive figures of speech and veiled intensities and hypothetical
> heroics naturally disappoint everyone. We have surely missed
> the point of our modern experience; the romantic interpretations
> of it [as in James] that have been given have not instructed
> us—or we would not be in such wretched trouble in general.
> If the fine art of writing is not to become an idle game, and
> reading a bad habit, all that has upset us must be rendered
> as such with an explicitness, a physicality, at which in marginal
> matters only, renderings of Worth dresses and Venetian scenes
> and talk in the grandest manner, James excelled (VII, 533).

What we need now from the writers, Wescott says, is "plain" talk,
a close and less "squeamish" examination of the realities of our
time. Wescott brings the essay to a close with an astonishing
instance of James's continued "moral" influence: he implies,
rather than argues, that D. H. Lawrence is like James in that his
interpretation of modern experience is essentially romantic; and,
as such, it fails to instruct us adequately because it still smothers
and obscures the basic realities.

As a mode of critical discourse this essay is peculiar in the
extent to which it is always and insistently personal: it is impressionistic rather than systematic formal criticism because such
power as this essay has derives from no systematic theory of
literature or coherent methodology but from the intuitions, impressions, and experiences of Wescott himself. But it is a very
rigorous kind of impressionistic criticism; Wescott did not just
sit down and rip off an essay on his impressions of Henry James:
the essay is carefully, even meticulously organized, but again
according to a rather peculiar scheme, beginning as it does with
a detailed personal anecdote about Wescott's own intense early
experience of James which is almost confessional in the sense
that Wescott brings in his inherently incestuous love for his
sister, his early but subsequently "reconditioned" effeminacy,
the "delicate" health of his sister, and even the unabashed tears
of adolescence. The unity of the essay does not derive from an
applied theory or methodology, nor does it derive from some

structural, stylistic, thematic or developmental center of Henry James; it derives from Wescott, finally, and in the same way that the unity of *The Grandmothers* and *The Pilgrim Hawk* derives from Alwyn Tower.

This essay (and others like it) is the expression in prose of the lyric mode Wescott used with such success and originality in his fiction. The essential difference between the two is that Wescott speaks in the essays in his own voice, without any need to invent a disguise and under no compulsion to fabricate a plot or other such details as would be necessary in a fiction. He can use himself and his own experiences directly as the source of his material and he can give them a form that is apparently natural to him. The lyric essay is ideally suited to Wescott's needs, just as it is to those of E. B. White, because it permits him to do the three things which he has always done best. A lyric essay is essentially a movement or movements of the self, and its real subject is the activity or process of perception, not in the abstract, but in an approximation of the complexity and detail of an actual experience where the images and truths not only intermingle but are equal. The three realities—the images, the truths, the activity of the perceiving self—can be presented simultaneously and, what is almost more important in Wescott, directly, with great "explicitness" and "physicality."

The significance of the James essay is less thematic than formal; Wescott had made the same points at great length in *Fear and Trembling* and was to make them again later. But the form of the essay gave Wescott a mode of discourse which, had he chosen to use it as extensively as E. B. White, would have proved to be almost perfectly suited to his talents and needs as a writer. That he continued to use it after he abandoned everything else is again significant, for Wescott's practice was always to perfect a form and then move on to another; but from the mid-1930's on, his one persistent mode of discourse was the lyric essay. The end result of this long but sparing use of a single form was to be *Images of Truth,* a collection of lyric critical essays about prose fiction.

The abortive years were not all loss for Wescott. In 1939, what had appeared to be a period marked by repeated aborting and an unwillingness to try again, suddenly took on the qualities of a long period of gestation. In 1939 the creative springs began to flow again, and in the five years that followed, Wescott produced, with all the rapidity of the earlier creative period (1924-28), one excellent work after another in a variety of modes. At least two of these—"The Dream of Audubon" and *The Pilgrim Hawk*—are nearly perfect "children," but all of them were the work of a mature and disciplined talent which had apparently fully realized itself and was now ready to go on creating, at will.

CHAPTER 7

The Native Works of the
Imagination, 1940-1945

I

IN 1939 WESCOTT said that, finally, after all the years of restlessness and travel, he felt at home in America. Certainly the nature and number of the works produced between 1939 and 1945 indicate that Wescott had attained some kind of equilibrium which enabled him to create works with a clarity, symmetry, and serenity not found in any of the earlier stories, poems, essays, and novels. What was begun in the 1920's is completed here, and splendidly.

The works of this period may be divided into three groups: ballet libretto, prose fiction, and lyric essay. Two of the groups need to be subdivided: the prose fiction, which consists of two novels and two stories, may be divided into the Alwyn Tower fiction (*The Pilgrim Hawk* and the two stories) and the non-Alwyn Tower fiction (*Apartment in Athens*); and the lyric essays, of which there are two, may be divided into pure lyric essay ("I Love New York"), in which Wescott himself is the principal subject, and critical lyric essay ("The Moral of F. Scott Fitzgerald"), in which, as in the James essay, the moral of Wescott's experience of Fitzgerald is the principal subject. One of the works, "The Dream of Audubon," has no technical predecessor among Wescott's earlier writings and is thus an absolutely new form; since it has no successors either, it remains unique. Another of the works (*Apartment in Athens*) has only a very few technical predecessors, for as an objective narrative it represents a kind of fiction which Wescott always thought he should but never could write very well. For this reason, it is a kind of divergence from the main stream, even though it does show Wescott again mastering a particular form which he had thought about and worked at over a long period of time. The other works all have technical predecessors and are thus developments from deep roots; this is especially true of the Alwyn Tower fiction, which goes back to *The Grandmothers* and *The Babe's Bed*. Thematically, all are profoundly related to the previous works, for Wescott has always explored only a few themes and his vision has developed in a small, even narrow way—vertically rather than horizontally.

Though *The Pilgrim Hawk* is surely the best of these works and the one authentic masterpiece Wescott has produced, "The Dream of Audubon" is the most astonishing thing he ever wrote. It is a work of great originality and lush sensuous beauty; nowhere in Wescott's earlier work is there any indication that he could write such a symbolic fantasy. From the beginning he has tended toward symbolism and symbolic narrative, but there is nothing that could be called fantasy of the kind that one finds here. This is invented fantasy and not the fantastic distortions of truths and reality which were habitual with the bachelor in *The Babe's Bed*. To be sure, three of the stories in *Good-Bye Wisconsin* ("In a Thicket," "Like a Lover," and "The Whistling Swan") have an element of fantasy in them and are at least tonally similar to "The Dream of Audubon." But the first and last of these are realistic narratives, and the other is a symbolic nightmare narrative, dark and terrible in its implications.

"The Dream of Audubon" is not like these at all, but resembles some of Eudora Welty's stories in which she begins with a historical personage and mixes fact and fantasy to create a symbolic narrative with a strange, mixed tone. The precise quality of this tone is difficult to define, but it seems to derive from the purity of the fantasy, from the joy the imagination takes in such inventiveness. To modify a phrase of Kenneth Burke's, one has the sense that a work such as "The Dream of Audubon" is the joyful dancing of the imagination; such richness of invention for its own sake is very uncommon in Wescott.

Like most of the works of this period, "The Dream of Audubon" has a density of detail which makes it extremely difficult to discuss in a summary fashion without excessive dis-

tortion. Wescott's technique, as in *The Pilgrim Hawk,* is to
create two masses of precise detail: one is concrete in the sense
that it consists chiefly of sensory images; the other is more
abstract in the sense that it consists chiefly of meanings and
truths. In "The Dream of Audubon," the mass of concrete detail
predominates, and the meanings are usually suggested in asides
along the way and then concentrated in a brief rider at the end.
The profusion and power of the concrete detail are such that
there is very little teasing of the mind with symbolic meanings;
one tends simply to submit to and enjoy the accumulation of
gorgeous, non-realistic detail for its own sake—to experience the
work, in other words, as if it were a ballet and one had only the
colors, the movements, and the music to respond to. The fact
that the work is a particular kind of fantasy also tends to remove
it from the realistic level and enables, even encourages, one to
enjoy it in a purely esthetic way. In fact, one tends to pass over
the symbolic meaning, which is made very explicit at the end,
and to retain only the extraordinary and fantastic effects which
Wescott has achieved.

The work resembles a triptych: there are three main scenes,
one in the afternoon, one that night, and one the next morning.
These are preceded by a kind of prologue in which the scene is
set, and they are followed by a kind of epilogue in which the
work is interpreted for us by Wescott. The time is autumn,
about 1815, and the place is southern Louisiana. The historical
material which Wescott uses as his point of departure is the
"tradition, which may be true, that Jean Jacques Audubon was
the lost Dauphin, the son of Louis XVI and Marie Antoinette"
(361). The work begins with a remotely realistic scene which
shows Audubon at work supporting himself (which he actually
did) by giving dancing and fencing lessons and by doing
sleight-of-hand tricks. From this point on, however, the progression is toward the more and more fantastic. The second scene is
Audubon's dream of the execution of Louis XVI and Marie
Antoinette, followed by the crowning of himself as the new king.

The third scene is pure fantasy; or more exactly, it is elements
of scenes one and two all mixed up and combined with new
elements to produce fantasy. The local characters who appeared
in scene one are replaced by birds who resemble them, and all
the birds are either extinct or nearly extinct species. Indians are

introduced into the scene as additional examples of wilderness creatures who have been partially or totally extinguished. Then the execution and crowning of scene two become the crowning and extinction of various kings and queens of the wilderness. The whole last scene is a fantastic and brilliant coronation-execution ballet which concludes with a recessional in which the whole weird group disappears into the forest as the sun rises. This is followed by a brief interpretation of what Wescott calls "a kind of feeling or meaning or double meaning" which the work expresses.

Among these meanings Wescott lists "the sadness of our despairing of Europe, as we can scarcely help despairing in 1940. The joy of our love of country. . . . the sadness of the harm we have done in our country. . . . and the hunter's devotion to whatever he has happened to choose as his prey" (374). He concludes with the generalized symbolic meaning of the ballet: "we are all hunters; and our heart's desire, whatever it may be, is always somehow a thing of air and wilderness, flying away from us, and subject to extinction in one way or another"[1] (374). No doubt the work does express all of these things in a remote way, but these abstractions do not really summarize the truths of this work; they do not lie in its correspondence to an external reality, but in the purity and beauty of the formal effects Wescott achieves, and these are primarily a matter of sustained stylistic enchantment.

In spite of its remotely somber implications, "The Dream of Aubudon" is a joyful work; it is the creation of an imagination which feels at home with itself and its material. In this sense, it is a native work of the imagination, organic to it and born of it naturally as a true act of creation. It represents the kind of original and excellent work which Wescott, had he so wished, could have produced in profusion from this point on in his career. That he didn't, couldn't, or wouldn't is what gives his development its peculiar curve, with its early, quick and spectacular rise, followed by an early, equally quick and spectacular drop, followed by a second sudden brief rise which was certainly higher than the first, followed again by a second sudden drop which was deeper and longer than the first, with another different kind of rise apparently in process, but with the end still in doubt. It is perhaps fitting, then, that his greatest work—

the native work of his imagination—should be about his own development as a writer: read in the context of his other works, this is certainly the central subject of *The Pilgrim Hawk.*

II

The Pilgrim Hawk almost has to be read in the context of Wescott's development because of the complex relations between it and his earlier and later works.[2] Just as *The Grandmothers* was a sequel to *The Apple of the Eye,* so *The Pilgrim Hawk* is a sequel to *The Grandmothers.* The three novels constitute a kind of trilogy in which Wescott has written a symbolic auto-biography of himself as a person and as a writer. In spite of the only use Wescott ever made of the first-person point of view in his fiction, *The Pilgrim Hawk* is not radically different in technique from Wescott's earlier fiction but rather carries to perfection certain techniques of prose fiction which one can find as early as *The Apple of the Eye* in the "Dan Alone" section and then trace through *The Grandmothers,* at least half of the stories in *Good-Bye Wisconsin,* and the whole of *The Babe's Bed.* And finally, every one of Wescott's major themes appears in *The Pilgrim Hawk,* with some new additions and some resolutions of conflicts not achieved earlier.

Like *The Grandmothers, The Pilgrim Hawk* is a retrospective fiction; but the situation from which it is narrated is almost exactly the reverse of the one in *The Grandmothers.* Set in America in 1940, the novel is about a sequence of events which took place during one day in "May of 1928 or 1929" in France. The first person narrator is Alwyn Tower, who is also one of the principal characters in the story he tells. As in *The Great Gatsby,*[3] the time lapse between the sequence of events which con-stitutes the plot and the time of narration sets up at least two primary time levels in the work and makes it possible for Alwyn Tower to show himself meditating on the characters and events as they unfold, and then to meditate and comment retrospective-ly on his own earlier observations and meditations. As the work unfolds, then, a double time structure is established, and the work moves forward always on two levels. Since there are many flashbacks within the one long flashback which gives the novel its plot, the work often moves forward on more than two levels and thus has a very complex time structure.

After establishing the two time levels, Alwyn Tower sets the specific scene, which is the house of Alexandra Henry, a "great friend" of his who is now (1940) married to his brother; Alwyn then begins the narration of the sequence of events with the arrival of the Cullens and Lucy, the pilgrim hawk. The last scene of the novel is a conversation between Alwyn Tower and Alexandra Henry shortly after the departure of the Cullens, so that the novel proper, which began in the present (1940), ends in the past with the last significant event which occurred on that day in May of 1928 or 1929. Once the narration of the main events in the past begins, it proceeds in chronological order, though the novel itself does not; for, in addition to the secondary flashbacks, Alwyn Tower interrupts, breaks, and stops the flow of his own narrative to comment on, interpret, and meditate on the characters, the events, and himself. This technique gives the work another kind of double and sometimes triple structure, for the horizontal movement of the work—the narration of external events—is constantly broken by vertical movements of Alwyn Tower's mind. These vertical movements are of two kinds: those which occurred in the past while the events were actually happening and those which occur in the present while Alwyn Tower is narrating. The whole novel moves forward then in a very dense and complex (but never confusing) way as Alwyn Tower shuttles around from external to internal, from present to various points in the past, and from one kind of comment to another.

The sequence of events which gives the novel its plot is divided into seven major and many minor events. The first major event is the arrival of Mr. and Mrs. Cullen with Lucy, the pilgrim hawk, and Ricketts, their chauffeur; it includes a long conversation in the living room between the Cullens, Tower, and Alex, which is mostly about the hawk and falconry. At the end of this scene, Lucy bates—that is, makes a futile effort to escape her domestication—for the first time, and what may be called the bating pattern begins. The second major event is a walk taken by the main characters. The movement from indoors to outdoors (or, more precisely, from domestication to nature) begins a pattern and a contrast which is continued throughout the novel. The third major event is the feeding of Lucy, and it is here that what can be called the hunger pattern is begun. Before Lucy eats, she again bates, and then defecates, which is part of the hawk pattern; and, like everything about Lucy, these acts are interpreted symbolically by Alwyn Tower. The fourth major event is the cocktail hour, which consists almost equally of a long conversation between Mr. Cullen and Alwyn Tower and of Alwyn's meditations on drunkenness. During this scene, Lucy is weathering in the garden, and Mrs. Cullen and Alexandra Henry are off somewhere else. The fifth event is the freeing of Lucy by Mr. Cullen in a fit of jealous rage—that is, he also bates—and the retrieving of Lucy by Mrs. Cullen.

At this point in the novel, the subplot, which concerns the three servants (Ricketts, and Alex's married couple, Jean and Eva) also moves toward a crisis, for Ricketts and Eva have been flirting and Jean bursts into a jealous rage, threatening violence. At the end of this scene, the Cullens, who had been invited for dinner, depart prematurely because of the two outbursts of jealousy. The sixth major event is the shooting in the Cullens car just after they have started for Paris. The event is deliberately confused, and one does not know whether Mr. Cullen attempted suicide or whether he tried to murder Ricketts, whom he regards, like Lucy, as a rival. That he attempted a violent and final act—bated a second time—is the important thing, for the whole novel moves toward and away from this potentially terrible event. Again, it is Mrs. Cullen who retrieves the situation: she immediately senses what is happening; deflects the revolver so that the bullet goes harmlessly aside; takes the gun from Mr. Cullen; and, with Lucy still on her arm, comes back to the house, goes out into the garden, throws the revolver into the pond, and, after explaining what happened to Tower and Alex, returns to the car and resumes the trip to Paris. During this scene, Lucy bates for the third and last time; and, while Mrs. Cullen is calmly getting her back up on her perch, Alwyn, shocked by the events he has just witnessed, is brought down out of his tower of meanings and finally begins to see the events, the people, and himself for what they are. The last event is the conversation between Tower and Alex Henry and includes, in the background, the happy sounds of Jean and Eva making up after their quarrel.

But this summary of the events gives no sense of what the novel is about or what Wescott is really trying to do because the narration of events is further interrupted by flashbacks which very succinctly supply the reader with details about the earlier lives of the Cullens, Alexandra, the servants, and Tower, as well as about the ambiguous relationship between Tower and Alexandra. The result is a pattern of love-relationships or triangles of great complexity and subtlety which are all brought to a crisis in the course of the story. Furthermore, as the story unfolds and as the reader is gradually supplied with details about the hawk and falconry, various patterns of meaning are developed.

The bating and hunger patterns, for example, are but part of an enormous symbolic cluster built up, primarily by Tower but also by Mrs. Cullen, around the hawk. As the work unfolds, Alwyn Tower, up to a certain point where this process is suddenly reversed, constantly, compulsively, methodically, and somewhat morbidly moves in his frequent interior monologues from the hawk to its possible symbolic meanings, which he then applies to himself and to all other characters in the story. The hawk gradually becomes an analogical matrix around which Tower fabricates a dense mass of symbolic meanings. He does this in a manner that is exactly like what the bachelor does in *The Babe's Bed* until, like the bachelor, he is so detached from the realities of the situation and lost in a labyrinth of symbols and meanings of his own making that he is isolated in his high tower of abstractions. At this point, the events of the plot turn from interesting, even extraordinary, to violent and actually dangerous ones. The turn is so sudden, and the distance between these realities and Alwyn's fantasy of abstractions and symbols is so great that Alwyn turns with the events and starts his descent from the tower. He reverses the process of abstracting and symbol making, which had obsessed him up to this point; and he quite literally de-symbolizes the hawk—destroys, as it were, the whole hawk cluster he has created—and gradually moves toward a truer perception of the realities of the situation, the characters involved, and himself.

What Alwyn Tower has done is to catch himself, just as the bachelor did in *The Babe's Bed*, engaged in an activity which is natural to him but which he always carries to perfection, building such a tower of symbolic meanings that he finally becomes enchanted, infatuated with the process and the meanings themselves. The higher he goes in following this habit of mind, the farther away he gets from the "excessive details," the masses of "petty" facts from which he began and which he was trying to "compress . . . into an abstraction or two, a formula or a moral" (123). He perceives ultimately that the correspondence between the symbolic meanings, the abstractions, and the factual realities has broken down and that the whole process is really "a kind of inexact and vengeful lyricism" (121). When this happens, he begins to doubt the whole process and his own abilities to perceive and judge the realities and to arrive at truth. And this, he says, so long as he proposes to be a "story-teller . . . is the whisper of the devil for me" (121).

The whisper of the devil is the fear that for Alwyn Tower everything is "inexact and vengeful lyricism"; that is, the meanings which Alwyn Tower thinks he sees in things are not really in the things themselves but are transferred from Alwyn to the things in an effort to make life mean something. When he begins "entirely" to "doubt" what he calls his "judgment in moral matters" (121), he is left with a nightmare absurdity in which everything is a self-projection. Wherever he looks, as if he were in a hall of mirrors, he sees "cartoons" of himself instead of true images of external reality. Alwyn is saved from madness—from taking the distortions as the realities—by first catching himself in his "vengeful lyricism," then by recognizing as absurdities the meanings he has spun out of himself; then by de-symbolizing, de-abstracting the hawk, the Cullens, Alex Henry, and himself; and, finally, with a certain amount of grim irony, by laughing at himself and what he has done.

By the end of the story Alwyn has come down from his tower —the very tower, in fact, from which the whole of *The Grandmothers* is narrated by an earlier, younger Alwyn—and has decided to stay on the ground, close to the petty facts. Alwyn Tower as an artist has become an absurdity, a man who can't shake the "whisper of the devil." And *The Pilgrim Hawk*, which imitates the artist creating and then destroying what he has created because one part of himself plays devil's advocate and whispers, "lies, all lies," is really Wescott's good-bye to fiction and to himself as novelist. Without absurdity, it can be said that Wescott slays himself as an artist in this work. And with cruel irony, for his is the voluntary descent of the artist from a relatively high tower which it took him twenty years to climb.

Whatever one says of *The Pilgrim Hawk,* the excellence of it, especially the great formal beauty of it as a particular kind of prose fiction, cannot be denied.[4] One can say, as some critics have, that it has a peculiar aridity because of the excessive symbolic loading on the part of Alwyn Tower through the first three quarters of the work; but, in a sense, to say this is to miss the whole point of the novel, for the hawk is deliberately loaded with meaning in order that it may be dispatched to carry off, as it does, one part of the self. The novel is not just about the loading of the hawk; if it were, it would have no resolution. What the novel charts is a completed process, the last step of which is the unloading of the loader himself, Alwyn Tower, who had been Wescott's fictional disguise for thirteen years. All the pithy aphorisms in the first three quarters of the work, and the heavy burden of meaning placed upon the hawk are finally seen as absurd, even comic, by a later Alwyn Tower and are either cancelled or reduced to half-truths.

The center of the story is, therefore, not the hawk and the hawk cluster but Alwyn Tower and his painful purgative movement toward the truth about himself. The movement is extremely painful because the hawk cluster is a brilliant, beautifully complex symbolic construct and all the aphorisms, so elegantly phrased, sound final and true. It is difficult to relinquish these creations because there is a certain exaltation that comes from the perception and fabrication of so intricate a set of meanings and of such beautifully phrased generalizations. But Alwyn Tower does so; and, in so doing, he completes the pitilessly realistic examination of his earlier, expatriated self by his later self.

The double point of view and the double and sometimes triple time structure are not technical tricks, as they sometimes are in Conrad; they are functional techniques: much of the force of the story comes from the reader's realization that a later self is examining an earlier one in action to show why it was rejected. Like so much of Wescott's best work, the novel is confessional: there is a brutal and painful honesty about it, as well as a sadness; the work is not about why a man couldn't write any more novels, but about why he wouldn't—why he silenced himself as a novelist for fear of not telling the truth. The commitment to truth was much more powerful than the compulsion to confession in fictional form; only the terrible condition of the Western world during the World War II and Wescott's powerful conviction that he had some truths which might be of use to the public caused him to break this silence and to write his didactic last novel, *Apartment in Athens*.

III

In many ways, it was really World War II which either shocked Wescott into writing fiction or acted upon him in some way to start him writing again. Every one of the fictional or creative works which he produced from 1940 through 1944 is directly or indirectly related to the war, and one of them is actually a war novel. The two Alwyn Tower stories which Wescott wrote between *The Pilgrim Hawk* and *Apartment in Athens* are, like the former work, about European experiences; and each contains its particular truths which Wescott felt would be relevant and useful to an understanding of and perhaps even a solution to the immediate problem of the war. The first of these, "Mr. Auerbach in Paris," is about a series of events which took place in 1923, mostly in Paris. But the story is primarily a portrait of Mr. Auerbach by Alwyn Tower, and its purpose is to convey through Alwyn Tower a short-sighted and mistaken attitude toward the Germans on the part of the Germans and German Jews which led to World War II. A subsidiary point is also made about the condition of France and the problems it will have to face after the war.

Hardly a story at all, "Mr. Auerbach in Paris" exists almost entirely to convey the truths mentioned above; Alwyn Tower's function is that of perceiver and conveyor—he is simply a fictional mouthpiece for Wescott. The story could easily have been written in the first person as an essay without any loss. The second story, "The Frenchman Six Feet Three," also narrated from the first-person point of view by Alwyn Tower, has essentially the same aims, but it is longer and much better than the first. Like "Mr. Auerbach in Paris" and *The Pilgrim Hawk*, this story is a retrospective narrative: it is set in America around 1942 but is mainly concerned with events which took place in 1938 in and around Paris. The story is very close to *The Pilgrim Hawk* in technique; Alwyn Tower is used to establish a point of view and then to complicate it with ironic perceptions and ambivalent reactions, some of which are made possible by the two time levels, one immediately before and one immediately after the fall of France, and some by the nature of Alwyn Tower as a character.

The story is primarily about France, the sadness of her fall from greatness and some of the causes for that fall; however, it is not just an excuse to get certain truths stated but is an attempt to dramatize the situation, to render in concrete human terms the sadness of France's plight and to embody in an individual Frenchman and in a confrontation between individual Americans and Frenchmen some of the causes of that plight. A post-*Pilgrim Hawk* Alwyn Tower is used to perceive and convey the true complexity and pitiable irony of the situation rather than to abstract and oversimplify it. At one point, for example, Alwyn has begun, as is his habit, to reduce the Frenchman to a symbol of France; but, remembering the lesson of *The Pilgrim Hawk*, he quickly reverses himself and moves toward a perception of the personal plight of this Frenchman, who, it is true, was somewhat lazy and complacent, but who is broken-hearted just the same because of what was happening to his country.

Though this story does have its truths to convey, it is not a didactic work in the way that "Mr. Auerbach in Paris" and *Apartment in Athens* are. It is the only post-*Pilgrim Hawk* story in which Alwyn Tower appears, and its importance derives from this fact. But Wescott did not publish any more Alwyn Tower fiction; instead, he turned more and more to the lyric essay in which he could work, in much the same way as he worked in these stories and in *The Pilgrim Hawk*, but without the burden of the disguise—without even the pretense of fictional deception. Alwyn Tower becomes his creator and is absorbed back into the artist who invented him. With the exception of *Apartment in Athens*, Wescott henceforth speaks in his own voice.

IV

Aside from the two essays published during this period, both of which will be discussed later with others of their kind, the last work of the period and the final fiction (to date) of Wescott's career is *Apartment in Athens*. This novel is bound to all of Wescott's other creative works of this period by being centrally concerned with World War II, but it differs from all the other fictional works because it is an "outside" narrative: told from the omniscient third-person point of view, it is from beginning to end an invented (rather than an autobiographically based) story. It is set in Greece during the German occupation, with no double setting or multiple time levels, with no technical tricks at all, for that matter; it is written in a straightforward, almost homely style and in a manner that is best described as extremely realistic. The realism comes primarily from the extraordinary amount of petty, everyday detail, the day-by-day developments in the life of a rather ordinary middle-aged couple and their children. Like most of the other works of this period, and nearly every work Wescott has written, the basic movement is toward knowledge, so that the work exists primarily for the truths which it contains.

In fact, the work was written, Wescott said, as his contribution to the war effort after he found out that he could not serve in the armed forces. And it was written, he said, because he thought he had something of importance to say about the Germans and the deeper issues of the war. The motives for writing the novel thus resemble those which twelve years earlier had produced *Fear and Trembling*. Like the book of essays, the novel is propagandistic; and, though the method employed to propagandize is entirely different, many of the truths are the same.

For the central theme of the novel, however, one really has to go all the way back to *The Apple of the Eye*. The central point of Wescott's first novel is that Puritanism, like all other codified theories of human behavior, has a disastrous effect on the individual self and society as a whole because it denies the reality of certain fundamental motives in man and promotes, even demands, the evasion of experience by theory. The fruit of such a theory is not only rotten but poisonous, as Wescott attempts to show in what happens to Rosalia in the novel. Such a theory does not accurately reflect experience but, like Alwyn Tower, reduces it to a set of moral abstractions; and such a theory does not encourage the self to seek out the experiences which it needs for growth, but either keeps it from them or renders the self incapable of enjoying them, usually by paralyzing it with guilt.

The connection between *The Apple of the Eye* and *Apartment in Athens* is to be found in the similarities between Puritanism and fascism. Though one is essentially religious and the other political, both are authoritarian, codified theories of human behavior which, according to Wescott, have disastrous effects on the individual and society. As Wescott presents it in the novel, fascism is a kind of secularized neo-Puritanism, but more extreme and ultimately much more terrible: it is an abstract, visionary, futuristic, political theory which rejects the concrete for the abstract, the real for the visionary, the present for the future, the private for the public life, the individual for the nation, and the family for the state. Like all such theories, it is essentially dehumanizing and representative of everything which Wescott abhors and has written—almost preached—against from the very beginning.

Like Joyce, Lawrence, and E. M. Forster before him, and Orwell as well as many others after him, Wescott sees this conflict as the central problem in the modern world. *Apartment in Athens* is not just the transplanting of Puritanism to Greek soil, or the serving of old regional wine in European bottles; it is an attempt to present in fictional terms a profound and, as things have turned out, true perception of what was to be won or lost in the war. The positive values—which were and still are in danger of being lost—are embodied in the novel in the Helianos family specifically and in the Greek way of life generally; and the negative values—the destroying forces present then as now—are embodied specifically in such people as Kalter and von Roesch and generally in the Nazi German way of life.

There are none of Alwyn Tower's tricks in this novel; it is all written on the ground as objectively as possible in a traditional but powerful way. In style and in other matters of technique it is a kind of plain chant in praise of the private, homely virtues. Like *The Grandmothers*, the novel is primarily

GLENWAY WESCOTT

a family chronicle and portrait; and, as in the "Bad Han" part
of *The Apple of the Eye,* it is "saints" whose lives are chronicled
and whose portraits are painted. The two saints are Mr. and
Mrs. Helianos; like all of Wescott's saints, they are sometimes
simple and foolish but nonetheless admirable people who have
a clear if somewhat ordinary view of the positive values of life.
Unlike *The Pilgrim Hawk, Apartment in Athens* is narrated and
developed in a way designed to place and to keep all the
emphasis upon the story being told and upon the truths toward
which the whole narrative moves.

The narration and development of the novel are simple, direct
and effective, especially throughout the last quarter, which must
rank among the best things Wescott ever wrote. The novel begins after Greece has been occupied by the Germans and with
the billeting of Major Kalter in the Helianos' apartment. Kalter
takes the best rooms in the apartment and quickly reduces the
Helianoses to the status of servants—or, more accurately, slaves.
The first part of the novel shows how the Helianoses passively
endure this intolerable situation, gradually solidify as a family,
and slowly, in their passive suffering, affirm the simple humane
virtues (the Greek way of life) which they come to represent as
the novel unfolds. The first major turn of the novel comes when
Kalter goes home on leave and finds that his whole family has
been wiped out at home and on the various fronts. He returns
humanized by shock and personal suffering, and he begins to
behave toward the Helianoses in a kind, even thoughtful, com-
passionate way. Mr. Helianos and Kalter have long conversations day after day on a variety of subjects, but principally on
Germany and Nazi ideals. During these conversations the
explicit conflict between the Greek and the Nazi-German way of
life emerges as the principal agon of the novel.

The second major turn of the novel comes when Helianos,
under the delusion that Kalter has really changed and is now a
person with whom he can discourse freely and openly, insults
Hitler. Kalter, whose deepest allegiances are really impersonal
and to the state, reports Helianos for his crime against the state,
and Helianos is imprisoned. The third major turn of the novel
comes as a result of Kalter's diabolical scheme for using his own
suicide as a means of furthering the goals of the state. He commits suicide because his grief—his humanity—has broken him,

and he is no longer useful to the state. Before his suicide, he testifies against Helianos to make sure that the Greek can be executed. Then he commits suicide in such a way that it will be possible to accuse the Helianoses of murdering him, his object being to provide the German police with a lever they can use to get information from Mr. and Mrs. Helianos about the whereabouts and activities of those Helianoses engaged in underground work against the Germans.

The last turn, and the great one in the novel, is the change from passivity to action on the part of both Mr. and Mrs. Helianos. This turn is preceded by a coming to knowledge, first by Mr. Helianos while he is in prison and before he is executed for refusing to give information, and then by Mrs. Helianos, after she has read a long letter (smuggled out of prison by the underground) from her husband in which he attempts to state what he has learned and what must be done. Up to this point, the Helianoses had simply endured, more or less passively; Mr. Helianos, however, becomes a martyred saint who died to preserve the Greek way of life; and Mrs. Helianos, at the end of the novel, joins the underground, determined not only to use the Germans instead when they attempt to use her but also to send her young son out to work for the underground as well.

The basic movement in the novel is from passive suffering to active work against the forces of tyrannical dehumanization. The move comes about as a result of two related pieces of knowledge: one about the true nature of the Nazi Germans; the other about the extent of their ambitions. The Helianoses (and Greece) in their relations to Kalter come to represent a potentially worldwide condition: the apartment in Athens is a microcosm, and the drama enacted there is about what could happen to every non-Aryan man, woman, and child dedicated to the private life and to the simple human virtues and pleasures thereof. Actually there are two kinds of drama here, one terrible and rather spectacular; the other, rather homely, often simple and foolish. The first is the struggle between the two ways of life; and the second is the drama of the private family life, the essential drama of living as Wescott conceives it.

The great affirmations of the novel and of all Wescott's work after 1930 are of this commonplace drama, with its daily trivia, multitudes of petty fact, and masses of concrete particulars.

These are the things for which Alwyn Tower gives up his spectacular high perch in *The Pilgrim Hawk;* it is for these very things that the bachelor in *The Babe's Bed* puts on a harness to curb the tendency which makes him distort and pervert, even lose sight of, the concrete particulars. Though Alwyn Tower is not in this novel at all, no part of *Apartment in Athens* could have been written without the knowledge Alwyn gained in *The Pilgrim Hawk;* for, what *The Babe's Bed* began, *The Pilgrim Hawk* completes. By the end of the later work Alwyn will climb no more towers, spin no further grandiose schemes, lose himself in no more labyrinths of symbols, engage in no further vengeful lyricism. *Apartment in Athens,* then, is a sequel to *The Pilgrim Hawk* in the sense that it is the kind of work bachelor Alwyn would have written, or at least have admired.

As Wescott's last published work of fiction, the novel has a special significance; though it is partly atypical in manner, it does represent the culmination of a long (twenty-year) development. It is a native work of Wescott's imagination in the sense that it contains and affirms most of the truths which, from the very beginning, he has subscribed to and attempted to convey in his works. It represents, also, the attainment of a goal he set for himself in the 1920's: it is, according to his own statements on the subject, a kind of ideal novel.[5] It has images and truths in abundance; it is narrated from the outside; it is impersonal; and it is an invention (but not a fantasy) which adequately conveys the images and truths. In short, it is the traditional novel Wescott had been trying to write since the late 1920's.

Fortunately, he did not succeed in doing this very early; so we have *The Grandmothers, The Babe's Bed,* and *The Pilgrim Hawk,* all of them original works derived from Wescott's own organic creative centers rather than from any traditional idea of the novel. These and "The Dream of Audubon" are the true native works of his imagination—genuine original creations in the best modern manner where the style and form of a work derive from the creating self rather than from external reality or any traditional form. Of these, *The Pilgrim Hawk* is the best and most original because it is an almost perfect realization of a style, manner, and form which Wescott created out of himself in order to express himself. For this reason, *The Pilgrim Hawk* is more organically related to Wescott and is closer to his center than any other work.

In style and form, *Apartment in Athens* is a deflection from this center, a willed work rather than a native one. This does not mean that it is an inferior work, for it isn't; some parts of it are as good as anything Wescott ever wrote. But it is something Wescott thought he *ought* to write, both as his contribution to the war effort and as a particular kind of novel. It is thus a duty work in both of these senses, which is perhaps why there is something mechanical and forced about it, as if his rational and moral centers kept driving him on to conceive and then to execute the work in ways that really ran counter to the flow of his creative talent.

No further fiction has come from Wescott since that time. This does not mean that he has not written any—he seems always to be at work on a novel—but that he will not release any for publication. With the exception of "Mr. Auerbach in Paris," all the creative and fictional works published between 1940 and 1944 indicate that Wescott has arrived at a level of mastery and achievement—craftsmanship—where it is simply a matter of selecting a subject when he wishes to do another creative work. Though his range has always been narrow, it would be absurd to say that he was written out. *Apartment in Athens*, a radical work for Wescott, even though it is a very traditional novel, certainly discredits that argument. Just what set him to creating again—surely the war was a key factor—and just what caused him to stop as suddenly as he had begun remain mysterious, or at least buried deep in the personal make-up of Wescott. The most plausible explanation is to be found in *The Pilgrim Hawk*, but no final or even partially final explanation will be possible until —if ever—Wescott's letters and journals are released and until all the aborted works are made available for study. That he kept on publishing, though in another form, is a tribute to his dogged staying power. And the fact that, after eighteen years, he published a book *on* the novel is something of a miracle of continued growth, for it seemed certain that he had given up as a writer.

CHAPTER *8*

In Search of a Form, 1945-1963

I

WESCOTT'S last fictional work was a genuinely public, even international act: it set the prevailing tone for his activities as a writer during the next eighteen years. His major development is from a writer of prose fiction to a commentator on it and, in a larger sense, to a public spokesman and worker for the arts and the artist in the contemporary world. Though no prose fiction or any other original creative works have been published since 1945, Wescott has apparently never stopped trying to write a novel that will match his idea of the perfect novel which he discusses at great length in *Images of Truth*. While he kept on trying to be a novelist, he also tried almost every other kind of prose endeavor.

His published works, exclusive of the material which was collected in *Images of Truth*, include three fine lyric essays, a retelling of twelve fables of Aesop which were published as a very handsome illustrated book by the Museum of Modern Art, miscellaneous book reviews, and many short pieces in the *Proceedings of the American Academy and National Institute of Arts and Letters*. His activities, as diverse as his publications, include private and public talks and readings, participation in various symposia, radio and television appearances, committee work for the Authors League of America, the Authors Guild, UNESCO, and the National Institute of Arts and Letters (he was president from 1959-62), and, most recently (1962-63), an extensive lecture tour.[1]

A peculiarity of this period is that almost all of the published work, including much of the material in *Images of Truth*, was either done on request or as part of Wescott's various committee duties. Some of the pieces are, therefore, perfectly routine, and the published work of the period has a diversity and spread which make it impossible to cover chronologically, piece by piece, as has been the practice thus far in the book. I have, therefore, divided the works and activities into distinct groups which will be discussed separately and related to each other and to Wescott's development as a whole. The groupings are as follows: (1) the three lyric essays, published in 1943, 1947, and 1959; (2) the *Twelve Fables of Aesop*, 1954; (3) the active work for various organizations devoted to art and the artist, but especially Wescott's long involvement with the National Institute of Arts and Letters, which began in 1947 and has continued to the present; (4) the miscellaneous book reviews; and (5) the formal and informal talks and lectures, the symposia, the radio and television appearances, and the recent lecture tour.

The last two groups may be considered first, for they require only brief discussions. The book reviews Wescott wrote during this period are important primarily because they represent one form of prose endeavor which he attempted again and rejected. The requirements of a book review render the form too constricting for someone of Wescott's talent and temperament. His criticism is all intuitive; personal; non-systematic; highly, even excessively subjective; and often written in a charged, sometimes finicky, usually highly emotional style. It is not that Wescott can't write good, brief, fair, and objective reviews: he wrote many in the 1920's and some during this period. It is primarily that the form is unsuitable for him. All of his creative life Wescott has been searching for the perfect form and for the form perfectly suited to his talents and needs; he has always been quick to try any form once or twice—and as quick to reject it summarily when he found it or thought it inadequate. One has only to read the Elizabeth Bowen review (1949) and then to open *Images of Truth* anywhere to see why Wescott would never be at home writing book reviews.[2]

The public and semi-private performances of various kinds represent another search for a satisfactory form of expression. According to Wescott's own account, he began giving semi-private and public talks to various groups as early as 1942 and has continued to do so ever since, usually on request, but most recently on his own initiative. One of the lyric essays—"The Best of all Possible Worlds"—and portions of *Images of Truth* were originally given as talks.[3] Wescott also participated, along with Kenneth Burke and Gilbert Seldes, in a symposium on the 1920's at the University of Wisconsin in 1962, part of which exists in a transcript.[4] Part of one of his talks—also on the 1920's—is available in typescript. He appeared on Camera Three, with W. S. Brown, in a program devoted to the late E. E. Cummings. And finally, many of the items published in the *Proceedings of the American Academy and National Institute of Arts and Letters* were delivered as brief talks.[5]

A handsome man who speaks with a slight British accent, Wescott was apparently born to talk: he is articulate, open, vital, informed, and enthusiastic. As in most of his published work, his own presence in a public talk is overwhelming; that is, one is always conscious of Wescott personally, not so much because he intrudes himself in an offensive way into the subject, deflecting the interest to himself, but because he experiences everything personally and presents it that way, using his own experience of the work or just his own experiences as part of his method of conveying the subject. His manner, then, is not really informal but personal. Like his dress and deportment, his manner is actually quite formal, even elegantly so; but the formality is softened by his warmth and enthusiasm. There is no boredom, no elaborate critical or methodological machinery; and no sense that one is hearing (or reading) a formal lecture. There is just the man who is discoursing on his own experience of a work, a subject, an author, a period of time, a place, and whose object is to convey, through himself, a sense of love for a particular work or author and the truth as he understands it.

This is precisely what he could not do, or found it difficult to do, in formal book reviews. Actually, the personal talk or lyric lecture or even symposium is an ideal form of expression for Wescott; and, when one stops to think about it, his recent lecture tour all over the country is not at all surprising. To put himself in front of an audience is to present the primary source of power and enchantment in all of his prose and much of his fiction—himself.

If he could write no fiction that suited him, at least he could go out into the public world and talk about it; and, further, he could, as he had done in the 1920's, again take an active part in the cultural life of his time. Both of these activities may be regarded as new forms of artistic expression which Wescott tried and successfully used in lieu of prose fiction: both show him in his role of public man of letters, a role directly opposed to the apparently almost exclusively private life he lived in the 1930's.

Wescott's long involvement with the National Institute of Arts and Letters began with his election to that organization in 1947. He also belonged to other organizations and acted with what he calls "some public spiritedness" in various capacities for them.[6] As the *Proceedings* show, the chief functions of the National Institute and the American Academy are to recognize and encourage excellence and achievement in all the arts at all levels. Since these have always been Wescott's own goals, for himself and for art in general, it is fitting that he should have worked in a public capacity for them and that from 1959-62 he should have served as president of the National Institute. According to the published record, which does not include all the committee work or other kinds of services, Wescott served the National Institute in a variety of ways: he wrote and delivered three presentation addresses (for Edith Sitwell, Marianne Moore, and Lincoln Kirstein); he delivered an introductory address for an exhibit of paintings covering the period from 1850-60; he introduced Robert Frost when he read for the group; he gave a reading, with Louise Bogan, of some of his favorite modern poems; he wrote a statement on censorship; he delivered an inaugural lecture upon being elected president; and, while he was president, he made the presentations of the grants and awards. In all of these capacities Wescott served in exemplary but idiosyncratic fashion: his encomiums are all characteristically personal and anecdotal, but to the point; and his inaugural address was one of his lyric essays or lectures, an involuted, intensely personal approach to and treatment of the problems the self (artistic or otherwise) faces in the modern world.

Save for the most routine of his activities, such as the grants and awards presentations, all of Wescott's work for the National Institute shows the private man in public action. The essential self is carried out into the world of public affairs with no apparent loss of integrity or commitment, with no need for or compulsion toward disguises of any kind; it has fixed on a permanent set of values, deep fundamental allegiances, and one sees it, not searching for new values but expressing and affirming the old ones in a new form or in a new mode of action. Some kind of equilibrium has been achieved which can be recognized in all of Wescott's work from *The Pilgrim Hawk* on. Presumably it is the equilibrium Alwyn Tower achieves when he comes down out of his tower and adjusts himself to the world as it is, or as he actually perceives it, when he gives up, once and for all, the vain, ambitious and hopeless dreams of his ancestors—that native land of the imagination which drove the pioneers westward.

Though this equilibrium did not preclude further prose fiction, it is a fact that Wescott, partly for reasons which are made clear in *Images of Truth*, now turned to other forms or modes of expression and action for the equilibrated self. A further mode or form which, as with nearly everything else he has tried, Wescott mastered and could have pursued at greater length but did not, is represented by *Twelve Fables of Aesop* (1954). This very slight but elegant and charming book was published in a limited edition by the Museum of Modern Art under the direction of Wescott's life-long friend Monroe Wheeler, and illustrated, very modernistically, from linoleum blocks by Antonio Frasconi. This kind of book takes one way back to the beginning of Wescott's career, for *The Bitterns* was privately printed by Monroe Wheeler in 1920; and after that *Natives of Rock* (1925), *Like a Lover* (1926), *The Babe's Bed* (1930), and *A Calendar of Saints for Unbelievers* (1932) were also printed in elegant limited editions, the last three by Harrison of Paris, which was run by Monroe Wheeler and Barbara Harrison.

Save for *The Bitterns*, all of these limited editions have been beautiful art objects, made for pleasure by a small coterie and designed to please a slightly larger one. They have a kind of purity about them and, taken together, constitute one center of Wescott's life and art. These books have seldom been frivolous or esoteric, but have been endeavors in which at least three and sometimes four people (publisher, printer, writer, and illustrator) have combined their talents to produce a personal book which is excellent, elegant, and beautiful in every possible way. These books are always numbered and signed, always printed on rich paper, usually set by hand, and always finished in such a way that they are a pleasure to see and read. They are, in other words, luxurious tributes to the principle of craftsmanship and beauty for its own sake.

But it would be a mistake to see these as nothing but useless adjuncts—as pure esthetic objects, ornaments to be possessed and admired. Wescott's commitment to the function of art as an image of truth or as an agency for the embodiment and transmission of truths is too profound. The beauty of the book is not meant to obstruct or even to deflect one from the truths it contains, but to enhance them. *Twelve Fables of Aesop*, for example, represents an effort on Wescott's part to convey certain basic truths in a clean, straightforward way. In fact, these "newly narrated" fables represent the attainment of an ideal for him; the mode of narration is the plain and simple style he used in *Apartment in Athens*, only it is plainer and even more direct. It is the narrative style he would like to be able to sustain for a whole novel. And each of the fables, as well as the twelve together, moves directly toward truths concretely presented and plainly stated. Without exaggeration, it is possible to say that the book represents in miniature what Wescott would like to have achieved in a longer narrative work, but he never has. Though he has said that the translation of truth-laden works would have suited him admirably, he has never published any translations or new renditions other than these twelve fables of Aesop, mostly, he says in *Images of Truth*, because he committed himself long ago to the creation of original works and has never been able to relinquish that goal, even though he can't attain it (24).

Here, then, is a further experiment with a new mode of expression; actually it is a triple experiment, for the fable is a literary form distinct in itself which Wescott, like Thurber, might have used had he been so inclined; the narrative mode is the kind Wescott greatly admired and might have adapted to a longer work; and finally, the concrete aphorism (the plain truth) embodied in a narrative and then stated in an unpretentious way is a combination which Wescott also admired and might have incorporated into longer fictional works. Again, all one can say is that Wescott tried these things, in a small way; carried out the experiment in a nearly faultless manner; and then dropped the whole thing to try something else—presumably, to go back to that perfect novel he had in his head somewhere.

II

Aside from the lyric critical essay, which will be discussed in the next chapter, the other significant form which Wescott experimented with during this period is the pure lyric essay. The great mystery is why he never wrote (or published) more of these extraordinary essays, for they are the non-fictional equivalents of *The Pilgrim Hawk,* pure organic works which seem perfectly suited to his needs and talents as a man and as a writer. These essays are, like *The Pilgrim Hawk* and "The Dream of Audubon," among Wescott's truly original creations. They represent real innovations within an established form—the personal essay; their roots are deep in American traditions, literary and otherwise; and they belong to a now clearly established modern tradition, probably best represented by the work of E. B. White.

The lyric essay is a hybrid form, somewhere between fiction or poetry and prose. Its salient features are found (1) in the nature of its structure, which always evolves organically from an experience or experiences of the self; (2) in the extent to which modern fictional and poetic techniques are used in a mode of discourse which is essentially neither fiction nor poetry, but prose; and (3) in the extent to which the undisguised self of the author dominates the essay, organizing it and providing the fixed center of values in terms of which everything is perceived and evaluated. For writers of a certain temperament, the hybrid lyric essay is an ideal way of translating the private life of the self into a public form and of using that self as a social instrument.

Wescott's pure lyric essays are intensely and sometimes embarrassingly subjective and personal, not only in their structure of detail but in their over-all structure, which derives from the peculiar jigs and jags of Wescott's meditating self. Though the essays are confessional in nature, Wescott is not using the public form or grammar as a confessional, nor is he attempting to transfer his own private burdens to the public. He has used his private life and self primarily for heuristic rather than narcissistic or purgative-redemptive purposes, to represent a fixed, even entrenched position, a profound commitment to a particular perspective. All of the personal, often very private, details are used to present, illustrate, and reinforce this position, which is that of Alwyn Tower at the end of *The Pilgrim Hawk* and which involves a commitment to the positive values affirmed in *Apartment in Athens*. The essays are a restatement and sometimes an amplification of the values to which Wescott committed himself with some kind of finality early in the 1940's; they do not represent any advance in the development of his vision; they are another attempt to create an ideal form in which to express his vision.

The three essays are about New York (or the city), the country (as opposed to the city), and the modern condition.[7] Some of these experiences are re-created in the most minute detail and then examined so as to make clear the epiphanal moment or moments which come at the end of many experiences. These epiphanies or truths are fragments of Wescott's total vision; each essay attempts to work through the concrete experiences of the private self to the truths of living which it has discovered. On the assumption that he is in some ways a representative self, the private epiphanies are offered to the public as equipment for living.

It is not necessary here to lay out Wescott's position—to enumerate and relate the values he affirms—for that will be done in the next chapter in the analysis of *Images of Truth;* but these essays and the four other kinds of endeavor discussed in this chapter do have to be seen in the context of Wescott's whole development. By the early 1940's, with some ideas from much earlier, Wescott's vision had set; he had achieved an equilibrium, a kind of peaceful balance, which is best seen in the firm and quiet affirmations of *Apartment in Athens,* but can also be found in all the works discussed in this chapter. When Wescott said that in 1939 he finally felt at home in America, he meant more than just a sense of belonging to his native land. When he finally relinquished New York in 1943 and moved permanently to the family enclave, he had made some kind of adjustment that surely represents finding, after all the years of restlessness and wandering, a spiritual as well as a physical "home."

All of the works of the years between 1945 and 1963 derive from this established center of being and for this reason have a certain finality, even serenity about them. The vision, limited now as it has been from the very beginning, has taken its final form and become a permanent perspective. Wescott's problem during this period was to find a form to embody and express this final vision; and to this end he tried, again as he has from the beginning, a great variety of modes of action and discourse, including (according to his own account) an enormous amount of unpublished fiction and other prose works. Two modes of public action and discourse emerged as dominant: the critical variant of the lyric essay and the public lyric lecture. These two were combined to make up *Images of Truth* (1962), Wescott's first original book in eighteen years and, in many ways, the most coherent and successful embodiment and expression of his vision. This will probably not be Wescott's last book, but it is an end-work in the sense that, believing he had failed at prose fiction, he created another form perfectly suited to his needs and talents and to the peculiar qualities of his vision.

CHAPTER 9

The Encircled Tower, 1939-1962

THE TITLE—*Images of Truth*—Wescott chose for the only book he has published since *Apartment in Athens* (1945) is wonderfully appropriate. It is a summing-up of the images and truths which he has accumulated since 1939 when the earliest of the essays collected in the book was published. Actually, the book goes farther back than 1939 because some of the truths which it proclaims, and the whole principle of concrete images as truths, can be found in Wescott's work of the 1920's. After forty years of movement and slow growth, Wescott has closed the circle of his development by producing a book which adds an unusual perfection to the symmetry of his life's work. The circle is the figure one should use, for it is from within an almost closed circle of known and fixed values that the book is written, and it is as the non-dogmatic (but assured) presentation of an established but idiosyncratic position that it must be treated. *Images of Truth* is a distillation, produced drop by drop over a twenty-three-year period in the still of a fixed self: it contains almost no impurities and has certain rich qualities which are not to be found in any of Wescott's other books.

The form which Wescott used for his summing-up, like the images and truths which he wished to present, is rooted deep in his self and came to fruition only after a similar long, slow growth. The eight essays on prose fiction are all essentially lyric; the key to their form is to be found in the title of Chapter Two: "Katherine Anne Porter Personally." The "personally" has a number of meanings.

Every essay, for example, is written in the personal voice, without disguises; and each is filled with personal anecdotes, details from Wescott's private life which are used as instruments of criticism, and direct applications to the life of the self as a test of value. Wescott is *never* out of the essays; he is the defining characteristic of the whole book and of the approach to prose fiction which the book presents. Coherent without ever being systematic, the approach derives its unity from the fixed self rather than from any formal principles of criticism or systematic theory of literature. The book is as much about Wescott, personally, as it is about prose fiction or the six authors he discusses at length.

But the essays are not delivered as autobiography, and they are not essentially confessional; Wescott has attempted to use himself—as he did in *Fear and Trembling* and as he used Alwyn Tower in *The Grandmothers* and *The Pilgrim Hawk*—to present and establish a point of view. He is engaged in this book, as he has been from the very beginning, in truth-saying; he has chosen to speak in his own voice, ostensibly about prose fiction, but actually about the truths and images of reality which he has found in certain works of prose fiction which he knows so well and loves with such an extraordinary passion that they have a profound personal reality for him. These works and the images and truths which they contain are so important to him that they have become inseparable from his life; hence it would be dishonest—a violation of the fixed self and its values—to separate them from his life, to eliminate the personal anecdotes, the private details, and all those other things which were part of the totality of his experience of the works.

In this sense all the essays are personal and written in what must be called the lyric mode. The form of the essays derives from Wescott's own multiple experiences of the subject, and these include personal letters from one of the authors, those from the author to friends of Wescott, meetings over many years with the author, repeated readings of the works, applications of the works to his own life, events which took place while he was reading the works and meeting the author or writing the essay, associational chains of memories, and simple reveries inspired by the author or the work. This multiplicity gives some of the essays what appears to be a very peculiar structure until one remembers that the center of every essay is the fixed self and its values and that every essay moves forward by excursions away from and back to this center. As one proceeds through the eight essays, it is really this fixed self and its values that one comes to know.[1]

Such power as the book has—in fact, that of all of Wescott's criticism—must finally derive from this fixed self and its values and from Wescott's ability to present both as persuasive. This self does not perceive in a systematic way; and its values, though coherent, will not add up to any theory. The chief virtues of this self are an immaculate, if idiosyncratic, mode of perception, which is often bewildering and occasionally tedious in the degree to which it fixes on small details; an unabashed and passionate personal commitment to the things perceived once an assent of the self has been made to them; a great facility for the rhetoric of personal commitment, for translating the essentially private and personal vision into public discourse; and, finally, a naïve earnestness about the importance of truth, reality and literature, the integrity and force of which one hesitates to question or to ridicule.

The book as a whole consists primarily of eight affirmations of the title: to an extraordinary degree, it is a catalogue in praise of the images of truth which Wescott has found in the six novelists and in prose fiction. But this is not all the book is: it also contains an idea of the novel which provides the book with its other center. The idea has a long history in Wescott; it can be found in the reviews he wrote during the 1920's and in all his subsequent writings on literature in general and on prose fiction in particular. In addition, the idea represents the kind of novel Wescott himself has always thought he ought to write and partially achieved in *Apartment in Athens*.

Images of Truth, then, considered in the context of Wescott's development, is more than just a collection of eight critical and personal essays on the novel and the truths which it contains. No one but Wescott (and perhaps his close friends) knows how many novels he conceived and aborted between 1945 and 1962, but the public record is clear enough: in lieu of novels Wescott turned to writing about the novel, specifically the kind which he wanted to write but, for various reasons, could not. Formulation, apology, affirmation, and praise took the place of original creation; the truth-saying, the creation of images of reality, the embodiment of his own vision in narrative art—in short, his vocation as novelist—were all transmuted and finally transferred to another mode of expression.

To anyone familiar with Wescott's career and development, *Images of Truth* takes on another dimension; it reverberates with his own inability to write that ideal novel which, ironically, seems to be quite alien to his own talent. The whole of the long, dense, and occasionally turgid essay on Thomas Mann, for example, could just as well be about Wescott himself; for someone who knows Wescott's work well, it is impossible to read it without making this double application. In fact, with the exception of the charming account of his call on Colette and Goudeket, all of the essays may be read in this way, with a kind of *double entendre* running all through the book. In spite of all the praise and affirmation, there is a melancholy sub-tone which emerges in the very first essay—"Fiction Writing in a Time of Troubles" —and increases as the book unfolds. By the end of the book, one's sense of Wescott's vicarious fulfillment is nearly overpowering; and correspondingly, if one subscribes to the interpretation of Wescott presented in the preceding chapters of this study, one is overcome by a great feeling of waste and loss. Irony turns in on irony as one follows Wescott's presentation and defense of his idea of what the novel should be and what is wrong with so many modern novels and novelists. He attacks again and again his own natural tendencies and the kind of novel in which he did his own best work. What this amounts to after a while is a profound self-denial. It is as if Wescott threw away the fine novels or short novels he might have written for the sake of the novel or novels he thought he ought to write but could not. He became a re-teller rather than a teller and not, it seems, for lack of talent, but for the sake of a fixed idea which ultimately is not worth one page of *The Pilgrim Hawk*.

Read at one level, then, *Images of Truth* is exactly what Wescott says it is on the dust jacket: it was written, he says, "to draw readers to books that I love, and perhaps to add a certain helpful, enjoyable perspective to their reading-experience; to give pleasure by various ways of writing in it, and perhaps, here and there, to convey something of my understanding of human nature and worldly wisdom, resulting from a longish and very fortunate life; and to state informally the general belief or creed of a writer for whom literature is a vocation, almost a religion, not just a profession or a livelihood."

The book certainly does all of these things, but a slight shift of emphasis is necessary if one is to understand Wescott's remarks properly. "Love" is the accurate word to describe his relation to the books he writes of, and joy or pleasure certainly describes the response to these books; but "helpful" ought to be written in capitals and linked by logical connectives to "love" and to what Wescott says about "conveying something of my own understanding of human nature and worldly wisdom." He loves these books for the images and truths which they contain; in fact, his whole book is really about a passionate love affair with various truthful fictions which have been helpful to him in his own life, either as verifications or instructions: it is an attempt to convey the paradoxical idea that fiction is, ought to be, and must be the greatest source of true images of human nature and worldly wisdom that we have available to us. This is the "creed" and the main reason why literature, especially the writing of prose fiction, must be a "vocation, almost a religion," a sacred calling in which the chief sin is to lie.

There is nothing new about his general creed; such additions or innovations as Wescott makes are all to be found in his distinctions between poetry and prose fiction and in what he says specifically about prose fiction. Due primarily, I think, to the decline of poetry as a public force, Wescott makes the novelist and the novel rather than poetry and the poet responsible for most of the truth-saying which literature is to do. In Wescott's mind, poetry seems to be associated with pure art, ornamentation for its own sake, and pleasure; but fiction, the highest kind anyway, is associated with truth and functional technical effects. Wescott seems to make a distinction between lyric and narrative which depends, as does everything he says about literature, upon the function of art as a vehicle for truth.

The highest function of literature is to mirror and interpret—reveal and instruct are his words—reality, by which Wescott means the actual physical and social world in which we live and the realities of life in such a world. These realities, as it turns out, are the simple, plain truths of *Apartment in Athens* and should be rendered with "prosaic simplicity, . . . brevity and explicitness," using "traditional themes and immemorial symbols and images." Such things as "brilliancy of ego, headstrong and headlong display of intellect, powers of elaboration, poetical afflatus, and that frenzied and exalted artistry which is like drunkenness" (7) are all peripheral and finally only distractions from the truth—forms of self-infatuation which Wescott invariably associates with poetry and certain disastrous effects which he feels poetry has had upon the art of modern fiction: he calls them "mere oddities and novelties of construction and style (. . . triangular armchairs and procrustean beds, three-legged trousers, and three-fingered gloves)" (16).

What Wescott desires in a novel is the truthful narrative, which he clearly associates with some traditional (really nineteenth century and older) "tried and true old notions of fictitious form" (17). He wants such a narrative form because he believes that "there is a more precise, potent truth in story than in philosophy. In a truthful account of something which has happened, our minds discover, almost without thinking, a kind of knowledge of the world which lies deeper and is less subject to perversion and change than all the rules of ethics cut and dried. The emotion of a story has a more pacifying, fortifying effect on our wild hearts than any amount of preaching and teaching" (19-20).

Although Wescott's idea of the novel is not really susceptible to rigorous analysis because it consists of a set of powerful commitments rather than a systematically worked-out theory, what he appears to be talking about in the above passage are the so-called concrete universals of art and the way in which they convey in a non-abstract way, as directly as possible, the truths of human nature and the world. Direct, non-abstract communication by means of such things as images, behavior, actions, and plot, with an absolute minimum of intrusive comment by the author, are among the chief characteristics of the ideal "truthful narrative" as Wescott conceives it. This "maximum impersonality," Wescott says, can only be achieved by means of a "disengagement" from the "autobiographical point of view," the "pride and willfulness and narcissism and excitability by which the life-work of most modern fiction writers has often been beclouded, enfeebled, blemished" (35, 36). Only by achieving this maximum impersonality can the writer escape the distortions of the self and approach the objectivity necessary for the writing of a truthful narrative.[2]

A novel, and Wescott here means the ideal novel, should be "a large lifelike portrayal of a numerous and representative society, with contrasts of the classes and the masses and the generations and the ethnic groups, with causes and effects in the private psychology of one and all, and with their influences on one another—every man to some extent a part of every other man's fate—and all of this made manifest in behavior, action, plot!" (46). Katherine Anne Porter's *Ship of Fools* is such a novel. Wescott calls it a "phenomenal, rich, and delectable book" and lists its qualities as follows:

> the hallucinating specificity; the supreme and constant mean-ingfulness of everything; the bewitchment of the story as such, or, to be exact, the stories (plural) interwoven; and a continual sense of cause and effect, both in the mind and in external circumstances, amounting to suspense but at the same time in-spiring confidence in the judgment and truthfulness of the novelist; the main generalizations of psychology and morality as plain and acceptable as the face of a clock, the minute hand seeming to cause the hours, the hour hand the days, and subsequently the weeks and months and years and indeed, in retrospect and prospect, entire lifetimes (49).

Wescott's idea of the novel—what it should be, what it should do, how it should be executed—is plainly stated in these quota-tions. Though all the passages are drawn from the first two essays of the collection, few significant additions to Wescott's idea of the novel—or, for that matter, to his general creed—would be made if one were to go on and quote from the essays on Maugham, Colette, Mann, and Wilder. The collection is reduplicating in its structure; it proceeds by repetition and amplification, more or less circularly round and round the same fixed points, reapplying them and adding new specific examples to illustrate them.

Such power as the book has is not in its intellectual frame-work. Wescott has no theory; his diagnosis of what is wrong with the modern novel is personal in the extreme and does not in any way take into account the achievements, including Wescott's, in that form in our time; his astonishing placement of Maugham

GLENWAY WESCOTT

at or near the top rank of modern novelists and his ranking of
Christmas Holiday among the great books of our time are never
more than arguments from personal taste. His long "attack" on
Mann for his lapses into "metaphysical darkness" (200) is, like
the diagnosis of what is wrong with the modern novel, personal
in the extreme and in no sense based on a systematic theory of
why abstract statement or prolonged philosophical discussion
cannot be part of a novel. The power of the book is all in its
nature as an appreciative endeavor: the eight essays are good
examples of criticism as an act of loving. Wescott's object is to
make known the beloved objects (a weak word for books which
have been transformed into living organisms by him after half a
lifetime of passion and devotion); and the method is detailed
commentary, which is seldom analytic but consists of enumera-
tions of qualities, plot synopses, profuse illustrations, repeated
effusions, and long exercises in the rhetoric of praise. The six
essays on specific authors move with the almost painful slow-
ness of love through the cherished details of the authors and
their works as Wescott has known them.

Considered at one level, without the complications mentioned
earlier of Wescott personally, there is a circle of joyful serenity
at the center of this book, a repose which is almost exactly
opposite to the restlessness one finds in Wescott's early life and
work. To use a metaphor which figures in all of his previous
work and reappears here as a trope for truth,[3] Wescott is at
home, where he belongs, with his family, with these truths and
values, with these writers and books. If he is not entirely at home
with his own creative genius, at least his highly original talent
for working in various lyric forms has partially realized itself in
these eight essays on prose fiction (albeit somewhat ironically,
when one remembers that the lyric novel is consistently "attacked" as an inferior form of narrative art).

That a man who wrote one of our finest short lyric novels—
which is full of truth in Wescott's own sense of this word, is
stylistically and structurally right in almost every way, and is
brilliantly original as a modern form of the narrative art—should,
in such personal lyric essays as these, so effusively praise the
somewhat mythical impersonal objective novel as the only truthful form of that art is indeed a towering irony. Alwyn of *The
Pilgrim Hawk* could hardly have topped it. The informed reader

hardly knows what to do with it once he has perceived this tower looming up inside the circle: the repose, the joy and serenity, the sense of a man in his sixties at home among familiar and beloved images and truths—all of these things are there in the book, powerfully and persuasively enough to send one to (or back to) the books which Wescott praises so highly and to make one consider seriously his circle of values. But what of that creative talent? Was it not, in the long dialogue which Wescott has carried on with himself since the early 1940's about the nature of his own narrative resources in relation to his idea of what a novel should be, talked right into self-betrayal? Was not this idea of the novel the real "whisper of the devil" in that circular garden, otherwise so peaceful, so serene? Or was it, in fact, as Wescott so frequently says in this book, not self-betrayal but self-knowledge: a realistic assessment of his own talent and resources which made him acquiesce to his own small destiny?

It is absurd to find fault with a man for the books he did not write; but it is also sad to witness what appears to be a long, mistaken self-denial, undertaken for an idea of the novel which is at best partial. There could never be only one idea of the novel; one cannot prescribe which point of view shall be used nor can one say categorically that an autobiographical point of view will necessarily becloud, enfeeble, and blemish a novel. It is in the nature of creative talent to transcend pro-scriptions, to create forms—as Wescott himself did—to embody a vision. The individual self, which Wescott distrusts almost pathologically, is as worthy and noble a subject, as potent a source of truth as most others. A novel does not have to be a "large life-like" portrayal of society, nor does it have to be written in the "plain" style which Wescott so much admires in the work of Katherine Anne Porter. Wescott's own idea of the novel seems finally to be so limited and limiting, so partial to a particular kind of novel with a very specific function, and to a point of view and style appropriate primarily to such a novel that he has excluded himself from his own field of endeavor.

Wescott has turned, over a long period of time, from the public practice of this art to discussions of it; the main reasons given by him for this change are that the nature and extent of his narrative talent render him unequal to and unworthy of the novelist's high calling as he understands it. About the nature of his talent Wescott is accurate enough: he correctly sees that he is inclined toward the lyric mode, dense symbolism, an elaborate style, and the interior life of the self—the images and truths, the slow, involuting narratives of the many Alwyn Towers of this world. His own problem, as he understands it, has never been a lack of subjects or of images and truths: it has been the problem of finding or creating the "right" form (15). It is true that from the very beginning Wescott wrote lyric poems which seemed like prose, prose fiction which seemed like straight factual prose, and essays which seemed like lyric poems or sometimes like prose fictions; that from the very beginning there has always been a mingling (not necessarily a confusion) of forms. His best work has never been done in the traditional forms; only when he has broken away from them and followed his own sense of organic form has he created powerful and original works.

The main line of Wescott's formal development in prose fiction is from *The Grandmothers* to *The Babe's Bed* to *The Pilgrim Hawk:* there is a rightness about the form of these three works that is lacking in *The Apple of the Eye* and in *Apartment in Athens,* both very traditional novels. Yet Wescott seems to regard *Apartment in Athens* as his major achievement in the novel; and, because of his inability to complete any more like it, he has relinquished the task. One cannot help feeling that it is really Alwyn Tower, his own fictional disguise and an authentic creation, whom Wescott has denied; yet Alwyn is still there, encircled by settled values, restless to be out. Wescott has domesticated his hawk-like self, for his own good it seems, so he won't die of frustration or starvation or take to pillaging because the prey is easy. But Alwyn hooded, perched on a well-groomed arm, occasionally bating in that traditionally and carefully furnished home, is a sad spectacle to anyone who has seen him in free flight and remembers the beauty of his movements and the strange ring of his cry.

CHAPTER 10

The Unfinished Tower

I

LITERARY HISTORY has many bins, and it is frequently the fate of minor writers to fill them with their works. Early in his career Wescott had the misfortune of being put into some of these bins and for the most part that is exactly where everyone has left him. One can find entries for Wescott in the indexes of nearly every book on the 1920's and on modern American literature. Turning to the pages indicated, one usually finds only a few polite but stale sentences or sometimes paragraphs on the Imagist movement, the little magazines, Midwestern regionalism, and expatriation. In these books, Wescott is treated as a minor writer who has already lapsed into history. It is true that Wescott's career lends itself to such treatment: he moved with great rapidity and ease through various phases of his development, and each phase was associated with one of these bins. After his one attempt at cultural criticism on the grand scale in *Fear and Trembling*, the nature of his work changed; and what he did (and did not do) could no longer be dropped into any bin. During the rest of the 1930's he fell out of the public mind, to be remembered, if at all, only in terms of the bins into which his early works had been placed.

When *The Pilgrim Hawk* was published in 1941, in spite of its originality, it was almost immediately recognized as a short novel in the best modern manner and dropped into that bin; *Apartment in Athens* is easily classified and put into the war-novel bin; after its initial success, it dropped out of sight. Until *Images of Truth* was published in 1962, no significant work and no fiction at all came from Wescott's hand to be put into any bin.

Again he fell out of the public mind, and his works became victims of the stale platitudes of literary history. *Images of Truth* and, I suppose, Wescott's long lecture tour have caused a minor revival: *The Grandmothers* and *Images of Truth* have been reissued in quality paperback editions, Wescott has appeared on television; and recently, described as an "eminent novelist," he had his picture in *Vogue* along with other "eminent" people who posed for a series of rakish fashion shots. However, someone will soon find a bin for *Images of Truth*—in fact, some reviewers already have. Because the work, though idiosyncratic, is a throwback to a traditional view of the novel, is essentially impressionistic as criticism, and is in no way a landmark in critical theory or practice, it, too, will soon be lost in the darkness of some bin. Such, it seems, are the trials of minority.

Wescott, of course, may yet surprise everyone; he is reputed to have trunks full of self-rejected material, most of it prose fiction, which he could revise for publication and which could, conceivably, help make him the "eminent" modern novelist someone at *Vogue* says he is. Given the facts, however, the term seems to have been used somewhat loosely: one does not achieve eminence by eighteen years of silence during the prime years when one has finally mastered the craft and has a vision worth translating into fictional form. To conclude this book with a long defense of Glenway Wescott as an eminent modern American novelist would be unwarranted.

Wescott's one authentic fictional masterwork, *The Pilgrim Hawk,* is or will certainly become one of our classic, modern short novels; it has the same perfection as *The Great Gatsby* and as "Pale Horse, Pale Rider." But one short novel is not enough. The regional novels and stories considered as a group constitute a significant achievement in that form; and in some of these—notably *The Grandmothers, The Babe's Bed,* and one or two of the stories from *Good-Bye Wisconsin*—Wescott was able to transcend the limitations of the regional form and to raise the works to a level where they may be read as something more than regional history or local portraiture. These works retain an intrinsic beauty and interest which is independent of their origins in regional experience and material. Wescott's other significant work of prose fiction, *Apartment in Athens,* though the last part is probably as good as anything he ever wrote, has a narrative tedium and stylistic monotony which saps its power. All of this does not add up to eminence in the field of prose fiction, but to a limited achievement; and one may never know whether Wescott had only one fine work in him or whether circumstances—personal and historical—combined to hold back a talent which it would be foolish to underrate.

Wescott has also worked many other fields: as a poet, a reviewer, an essayist, a cultural critic, a modern hagiographer, a librettist, an art critic, a sort of translator, a lecturer, and, over a long period, as a worker for the arts. Like such people as Kenneth Burke, Edmund Wilson, and E. E. Cummings, Wescott has tried a great variety of forms: he has sustained his efforts in only two of them—prose fiction and the essay. He has been as restless in his lifelong search for an appropriate form as he was in his early search for a place to live.

As I have already pointed out, Wescott achieved a certain limited excellence in everything he undertook because of his uncanny ability to master rapidly the essential characteristic of a given form; and, where a particular form happened to permit the full expression of his own natural lyricism, or where he could adjust a form to his needs or combine forms to create hybrid ones, he occasionally achieved a brief brilliance. For example, he wrote hard, cold Imagist poems and incisive witty reviews, a lovely, sensuous ballet libretto and terse aphoristic renditions of Aesop's fables; once he discovered how to adjust the critical essay to his own intensely personal and subjective, always essentially lyric approach, he wrote a number of first-rate lyric critical essays;[1] and, when he discovered how to do the same thing with the straight essay he achieved the same results in the lyric essay. But few things have ever been sustained by Wescott: one can add up the prose and the prose fiction and have something solid to work with, but the others won't add up in the same way and seem to indicate a restless talent easily bored once it has mastered a problem.

II

What is one to do with a development such as Wescott's and how is one to assess this minor writer in such a way as to arrive at a fair evaluation? A number of interpretations of Wescott's career have been advanced which ought to be mentioned but with the cautionary note that they were all put forward originally in the 1930's and that later repetitions of them do not account adequately for Wescott's publications after 1940. Moreover, all are based on Wescott's failure to fulfill the high promises of his beginnings in the 1920's.

The first interpretation is that Wescott was never anything but a regional writer and that, once he had depleted or moved away from his regional material, he was forever finished as a writer. This interpretation clearly has two sub-divisions: one is based on the idea that the regional matter provided Wescott with a ready source of fictional material and that he simply used it up, as one would an inheritance, and that, when it was gone, he was bankrupt as an artist.[2] In the 1930's this interpretation seemed at least partly valid; but later developments have proven it false, and the kindest thing to do with it is to dismiss it.

The second subdivision links the regional fiction with Wescott's expatriation and is based on the idea that Wescott's failure resulted from his denial of America and of his deepest native creative sources.[3] Again, later developments disprove this interpretation, for all of Wescott's work after 1939 (like all of the work before that date, with the exception of *A Calendar of Saints for Unbelievers*) is deeply, profoundly American.

The third interpretation is more persuasive and not so easily dismissed. It is suggested by many of the things which Wescott says about himself and America and is based upon certain obvious similarities between distinctly American traits of character and Wescott's career. Like that of Fitzgerald, Wescott's career is seen as a kind of parable of the American spirit: his bright youth, so full of promise and hope, so full of achievement and future expectations, never developed into a rich maturity. His failures are those of the American spirit, which is essentially youthful and tends to burn out at an early age, frustrating its own as well as others' expectations for it, and ending up, if it survives, in a bleak, bored middle age.[4] American literature is full of such burned-out talents, and it is neither difficult nor implausible to place Wescott in this class of writers from whom so much was expected and to use his career, as Fitzgerald's has so often been used, as a lesson in American cultural history.[5]

Aside from these three common interpretations, two others have been put forward. The first appears as part of an essay by Marjorie Brace, entitled "Thematic Problems of the American Novelist," which appeared in *Accent* in 1945;[6] the second is the basis of an essay entitled "The Maturing of Glenway Wescott" by C. E. Schorer, which appeared in *College English* in 1957.[7] Both of these essays make large claims for Wescott, but of opposite kinds: Miss Brace uses Wescott in the last third of her essay to illustrate its thesis about why the modern American novelist is usually a failure; and Mr. Schorer reverses the standard interpretation of Wescott as a failure and tries to show how in his development there actually has been a slow maturation of technique and vision and that, properly viewed, this development is a most instructive, even prophetic one.

Miss Brace is a thesis rider; she is also a very persuasive and witty writer, so one has to be careful about how much of her essay one accepts without the most careful scrutiny. The thesis has to do with the relation of the novel to society and with the function of the novel as a cultural force. The function of the novel, Miss Brace says, is to mirror and analyze the society of which the author is part. The dilemma of the American novelist is that he "cannot write seriously without alienating himself from the values of his society, and at the same time he cannot function apart from his audience" (*Accent*, VI, 48). The American novelist cannot accept his own social framework or morality because it would "mean an acceptance of a morality in which art had no place" (VI, 46); if he rejects it outright, as many writers have done, he is left without a meaningful social framework or moral element: and, though his work may mirror society, the reality of his novel is weakened, even vitiated, by the violence of his hatred and rejection. To accept such a social framework as one finds in America is a vulgarization of one's moral integrity; and to look elsewhere—to Europe, for example— for a positive social framework is an evasion of the problem. After citing many examples of these three, and other, ways in which American novelists have failed, Miss Brace comes round to what she calls the "vulgarization of the European theme," which provided James and others with so powerful a means of exploring, without vulgarization, the profound ambiguities of our moral, social, psychological, and esthetic life.

This theme is vulgarized by giving the "greatest value to the American perspective," which is exactly what she says Wescott has done in *Apartment in Athens*. "If his book is vulgar," says Miss Brace, "it is not by intent, but with the helpless doomed vulgarity that accompanies so many literary efforts to cope with circumstances of moral ambiguity." *Apartment in Athens*, according to her, is "peopled entirely by naïve Americans in European clothing . . . [and] has nothing to do with the real Europe . . . [but] only sounds our old chord: a timid negative striving for values against a positive bourgeois nihilism." Except in *The Pilgrim Hawk*, which Miss Brace says "is one of the most intelligently conceived and realized novels written by a contemporary American," and in portions of *Apartment in Athens*, when "the doctrinaire aspects of the book are forgotten, and the situation [is] narrowed down, *abstracted*, into a sort of diapason of good and evil, in all their polarized unity," Wescott has tended to create a "newspaper world" in his novels because he commits the "fatal mistake of trying to form an aesthetic pattern by making life itself appear less equivocal; and his newspaper minded audience is irremediably with him, understanding every word" (VI, 51, 52).

It should be clear from the quotations that Miss Brace has attempted to use Wescott as a representative modern American writer and all of his novels as examples of how the American novelist has succeeded and failed. At one point, she says that *"Apartment in Athens* is not interesting in itself, but only in the light of the author's entire work, a work that in its meagre but progressive exploration of every American theme is a kind of aesthetic pilgrimage, resembling nothing so much as a story Henry James might have written" (VI, 51). Only in *The Pilgrim Hawk* does Wescott succeed, and then only because of his use of Alwyn Tower as the American bystander who, "confronted by the density of European experience," can add "layer on layer of ambiguity" to the novel and without vulgarization (by which Miss Brace means oversimplification) provide us with an analytic mirror of "the dark inner realities of our alienation, and the conflict among egos that is our most menacing social problem" (VI, 52-53).

Occasionally *Apartment in Athens* also succeeds; when it does, Miss Brace says, it is because "Wescott's questing moral passion becomes pure, intellectualized, and his style takes on a cool rhythm that reminds us of an American accent of a different kind: the accent of our classics. In such passages Wescott recaptures the profoundly native voice, but only as his novel ceases to be a novel, and turns into a philosophic dialogue, a poetic discourse" (VI, 52). Miss Brace's final point is that "the failure of the novel" indicates "an accelerated social neurosis" (VI, 53), by which she means, in part anyway, that conditions in America are such that it is almost impossible for novelists to write authentic—what Wescott might call "truthful"—novels. What makes this point so interesting is that Wescott says much the same thing in *Images of Truth;* and, using himself as a representative figure, he offers it as one of the explanations as to why he has not written novels in the last eighteen years.[8]

The import of Miss Brace's remarks is that Wescott may be used as a small but remarkably clear mirror of the American novelist in the modern world. This is in part what Mr. Schorer argues, but on a somewhat larger scale and with quite different results. He is more complete in his coverage of Wescott's works; much more meticulous and just in his comments on the individual works (Miss Brace, for example, demolishes without pity *The Apple of the Eye* and says rather ignorantly that Wescott wrote nothing of importance between *The Grandmothers* and *The Pilgrim Hawk*); and in the end, I think, more suggestive and persuasive. In many ways, his essay is a model of what can be done with a writer such as Wescott, for Mr. Schorer has made an exemplary analysis of this minor writer and shown us many things which we might otherwise never have seen.

In his essay, Mr. Schorer charts and correlates the development of three things in Wescott's works: the settings, the recurrent themes, and what he calls the "characterizing symbol." The first novel, certainly the most immature of all the works, is also the most limited in its setting, which is confined primarily to rural Wisconsin. The major symbol is the marsh which, as Schorer points out, is generally successful, and the major theme —recurrent in all of Wescott—is that "to break the commandments," especially those governing the sexual life, "may after all be a permissible part of the good life" (*CE* XVIII, 321). *The Grandmothers* begins the widening of focus which was to continue throughout Wescott's development because it portrays life outside of Wisconsin and introduces the Europe/America-Wisconsin contrast. Alwyn Tower in this novel serves the function of the marsh in *The Apple of the Eye;* he is the principal unifying device, and he also carries on and deepens the investigation of the major theme. *Good-Bye Wisconsin* brings in still more of the outside world "by making the contrast between Wisconsin and Europe a dominant concern"; and the major theme—love and various kinds of sexual deviation as they are related to the individual self and to the good life—here receives its fullest expression. As Mr. Schorer points out, it is in *The Babe's Bed* that this phase of Wescott's early artistic and intellectual development is concluded. The themes of revolt, deviation, and rejection are resolved; and Wisconsin as a symbol takes on the significance of "youth's everlasting problem," which can only be solved by the self when it grows away from its "discontented ancestors into its own world" (XVIII, 322). Schorer then points out that "of equal importance with this maturing viewpoint is a new strategy of characterization which might be called the characterizing symbol, by which Wescott chiefly shows his progress as an artist. He employs a living creature, the baby in its bed, which functions to symbolize certain human traits, to illuminate the characters by their reactions to it, and obviously to unify the story in another sphere in addition to the plot" (XVIII, 322-23).

Schorer then charts with great astuteness the two kinds of deterioration of this hard-won maturity in *Fear and Trembling* and in *A Calendar of Saints for Unbelievers:* the core of *Fear and Trembling* is the maturing vision of the four regional works of fiction, but there has been a breakdown in the language and style; in *A Calendar of Saints for Unbelievers,* however, there is a deterioration of everything. *The Pilgrim Hawk* represents a remarkable recovery of all that seemed lost in the 1930's as well as increased intellectual and artistic maturity. In this work Wescott widens the focus still further by entering a "new international phase" which he was to continue in his next and last work of fiction. "In *Apartment in Athens* . . . Wisconsin is not mentioned at all, just as the outside world does not appear in his first novel" (XVIII, 324). Here, Schorer says, Wescott "has reached the extreme of his travel from West to East. At least, as regards literal fictional materials, his work totally abandons the region from which it sprang. It completes a trend of his writing with all the regularity of a linear mathematical equation" (XVIII, 324). Again, Schorer correctly points out, as he completes his charting and correlating of Wescott's development, that this novel, like the first, is very conventional in its structure and style, and lacks both the "characterizing symbol" and a unifying narrator such as Wescott used so successfully in *The Babe's Bed* and *The Pilgrim Hawk*.

The rest of Mr. Schorer's essay draws conclusions from and about this evidence. It would be foolish to attempt a summary of all Mr. Schorer's points, so I will mention only the most important ones which he makes about how one may justly interpret the development of Glenway Wescott. This development, he says, "clearly produced mixed merits: a gain of technical virtuosity, a loss of reality. In some ways like other American expatriates—one thinks, often, of James, Garland, Hemingway—his late works shows improved economy and centralization, drama and clarity, with a loss of local connections, memorable ideas, and vigorous characters. His last phase showed the clarification and cumulative enrichment of his artistry" (XVIII, 326). In addition to these remarks on Wescott's technical development, Schorer points out that Wescott's career "reveals the times" in at least two significant ways: the pattern of his development "reminds one distinctly of the dilemma facing the expatriates in the 1930's, as portrayed by Malcolm Cowley: "'they could go . . . back to Wisconsin, but only to say goodby. They had been uprooted from something more than a birthplace, a country or a town. Their real exile was from society itself, from any society with purposes they could share, toward which they could honestly contribute and from which they could draw new strength'" (XVIII, 326). And the pattern of his development

reminds one, too, of the new role America is playing: having out lived the days of self-reflective provincialism, with whatever minor notes of self-criticism, it now finds itself having to consider how to apply local American methods and viewpoints to the situation of a major industry in Europe or a farmer in Asia. With the abandonment of isolated bucolic American life for international guidance, haphazard individualism gives way to more systematically planned enterprise directed toward socially constructive goals. The change may involve some loss of the glamorous American freedom and prosperity. It may well be reflected in a literature of similarly modified characteristics. Wescott's career, a very model of such changes, has consciously wrought out this moral for a student of our life. If he in 1934 seemed a prototype of Cowley's socially alienated exile, he now stands as a suggestive indicator of our future (XVIII, 326).

III

That Wescott is, in what he likes to call his "small" way, a prototypical figure in at least the ways suggested by Miss Brace and by Mr. Schorer is too clearly demonstrated by his works to need debating. In Wescott's own development there is a miniature history of a great many significant technical and thematic trends and developments in modern American literature from 1920 to the present: Imagism and, in a larger way, the extraordinary recrudescence of poetry in the 1920's; the little magazines and the American culture and literature debate which raged throughout the 1920's; regionalism and the question of the native land and character; technical experiments in prose fiction, especially with point of view and structure; the emergence of the self as a major theme in prose fiction; revolt from established forms and values; exile and return, America versus Europe and the whole expatriate movement; cultural criticism on the grand scale in response to the economic and political ills which ravaged the Western world; democracy versus fascism, or politics as the emergent central concern of the serious novelist; the sense as well as the fact of times too troubled for creation; the turn from creation to speculation, from prose fiction to prose as a mode of discourse; an obsessive life-long concern with form, or what may be called the search for the appropriate form of expression; a belief in the transcendent importance of literature as an instrument of individual and social health; and, finally, a commitment to the private rather than the public life as an individual solution to a general problem.

All of these things may be found in Wescott's development, with some recurring, but with most appearing in the linear form which Mr. Schorer mentions. As Miss Brace and Mr. Schorer point out, Wescott has indeed moved with his times; and the extent to which his movements have had variety may be seen by contrasting him to someone like James Gould Cozzens, whose values also became fixed relatively early but who, once he discovered his proper form early in the 1930's, devoted himself, with almost no deviations, to the repetition and perfection of that form. Wescott's whole career, however, has been a continuous search for his proper form; thus, though his vision has remained remarkably constant since 1940, no two of his books, as he points out, have been alike. This gives his development a peculiar pattern; for, just as he seems to have found his organic form, he drops it and moves on. Like most authors, for example, Wescott was clearly on a double quest at least through *The Pilgrim Hawk:* in addition to an organic form he was also in search of a self and all that this implies. As is often the case, these two quests, both of which are endemic among modern writers, appeared to have been completed in *The Pilgrim Hawk,* but time has now shown that Wescott did not have the same kind of certainty about the form of that work as he did about the truths which it expressed.

To a really extraordinary degree, the positive values of the self have remained fixed for Wescott from 1940 on, but the search for a form has gone on. However, unlike many other writers, as the self became fixed in its values, it became less and less creative: from 1920 through 1940 (*The Pilgrim Hawk*) Wescott wrote nine books of varying lengths, a ballet libretto, plus numerous book reviews and essays; from 1941 through 1963 he has written three books, and the last of these (*Images of Truth*) is a collection of nearly everything he has published since 1945. Of equal importance is the fact that Wescott has published no fiction since 1945; this would suggest that, contrary to what almost everyone has said, the search for the self rather than the regional material was the motivating creative force. Fiction seems to have been an active and passive (retrospective) part of that search, something compulsive and necessary as long as the search continued. The basic movement in all of Wescott's fiction is toward knowledge for the principal character, whether it is Dan Strane, Alwyn Tower, the bachelor, or Mr. Helianos. Read in order, the fictional works present a completed search, the last stages of which can be found in *The Pilgrim Hawk,* with *Apartment in Athens* as a kind of rounding out or amplification and application of the values arrived at in *The Pilgrim Hawk.* The loss of vitality from *The Pilgrim Hawk* to *Apartment in Athens* is extraordinary; it is as if the source of power had been diminished. *Apartment in Athens* is a work of the will, almost of duty; it carries Wescott's truths out to the world, probably more clearly than any other work he ever wrote, but in an alien form and in a predominantly lifeless style.

If Wescott has now chosen not to make fiction out of his life, the decision is surely his own business; but it still seems like a grievous loss, especially when one considers that it resulted in part from the scrupulous but ironic domestication of the creative self for the sake of truth, when in fact the fictional re-creation of the life of that self was the most powerful, beautiful, and truthful thing Wescott ever wrote. Wescott's talent did not dry up or run out, any more, let us say, than Melville's or E. M. Forster's did; it was permitted to lapse, or it was shut off, or the need which drove that talent to the creation and completion of fictions ceased to exist. Whatever the reasons—and surely they are enormously complex and ultimately a dark tangle of mixed motives, some personal, some familial, some social, and some artistic—the results have been a curiously mixed career, not yet completed and thus still open to further development. At the moment and for the last eighteen years, Wescott's publications indicate a development away from fiction toward criticism, and the recent publication of *Images of Truth*—as well as the projected omnibus collection, *A Windfall*—suggests that there may yet be a significant late phase to go along with and perhaps to complete a development which until now has had only early and middle phases.

If there is such a phase and if Wescott is true to form, there might yet be two novels to add to the two early and two middle ones, which would require a reassessment of his achievement in prose fiction. As a poet, critic, and essayist, it seems unlikely that he will ever be anything but a minor figure, remembered only for such fine individual pieces as "The Moral of F. Scott Fitzgerald." His one sustained effort has been in prose fiction, but even here one has the same sense of incompleteness; for in full career, and surely at the very peak of his powers, when it seemed certain that, after the treacherous 1930's, he was ready to fulfill the destiny suggested by the name of his fictional disguise, Alwyn Tower, he abandoned the enterprise. The four novels and seventeen stories he has so far left us, all of them published between 1924 and 1944, tease the mind because nearly all of them promise and a few of them actually reach a high level of excellence. Yet his achievement in prose fiction, like his whole career, lacks a cumulative stature: with one exception, all of the towers he built are small; many of them have since been abandoned; and the whole structure, varied and intrinsically interesting though it is, remains unfinished.

Notes and References

Notes and References

Chapter One

1. The principal source for the biographical material is Sy Kahn's invaluable doctoral dissertation, *Glenway Wescott: A Critical and Biographical Study*, University of Wisconsin, 1957, hereafter referred to as Kahn. Mr. Kahn's main sources were Wescott himself, Wescott's family and many of his friends, and Harper & Brothers. I have mined this rich vein extensively, and am indebted to Mr. Kahn to such an extent that I sometimes feel guilty about it.
2. See Kahn, pp. 31ff. for another interpretation of Wescott's achievements as a poet. Mr. Kahn rates Wescott's poems much higher than I do and attaches more significance to Wescott's place in the Imagist movement. Yvor Winters, in *In Defense of Reason*, also feels that Wescott's experiments in poetry were much more significant than I do.
3. Like Ford Madox Ford, Wescott is given to the use of ellipses marks. After attempting and failing to devise a system whereby I could indicate unobtrusively when the ellipses marks were Wescott's and when they indicated an omission in a quotation, I decided to let the whole matter go. I have seldom omitted anything in the quotations, so most of the ellipses marks are Wescott's.
4. Kahn, p. 28.
5. Frederick J. Hoffman, *The Twenties* (New York, 1955), pp. 174-75. The whole of Chapter V, however, is relevant here.
6. Fred B. Millet, "Introduction," *The Grandmothers*, Harper's Modern Classics Edition (New York, 1950), p. x. All quotations from *The Grandmothers* are from this edition.

Chapter Two

1. For example, see Patrick F. Quinn, "The Case History of Glenway Wescott," *Frontier and Midland*, XIX (1938-1939), 12; C. E. Schorer, "The Maturing of Glenway Wescott," *College English*, XVIII (1957), 325; Kahn, p. 126; and Dayton Kohler, "Glenway Wescott: Legend Maker," *Bookman*, LXXXIII (1931), 145.
2. In Joseph Warren Beach's *The Twentieth Century Novel* (New York, 1932), Wescott is treated in a section called "Expressionism" along with Thornton Wilder, Waldo Frank, and many others. And in Harlan Hatcher's *Creating the Modern American Novel* (New York, 1935), Wescott is treated in a section called "Poetic Versus Hard-boiled Realism" along with Elizabeth Madox Roberts, Thornton Wilder, and Kay Boyle. See also Kahn, pp. 281ff.
3. Kahn, p. 73.
4. *Ibid.*

5. To my knowledge, this reversed Genesis myth is best seen in James Joyce's *A Portrait of the Artist as a Young Man*, especially in Chapters III and IV of the novel; but it is also to be found in Joyce's stories "A Painful Case" and "Eveline" and in E. M. Forster's first four novels.

6. *The Apple of the Eye, The Grandmothers, The Babe's Bed,* and *The Pilgrim Hawk* may certainly be read as fictional or symbolic autobiography with very little forcing. One has only to read Kahn, Wescott's own autobiographical notes and essays, and the many confessional remarks he makes in his other essays to discover the extent to which these works are autobiographically based and render a fictional account of Wescott's own life.

7. Kahn, p. 85.

Chapter Three

1. See "Show Mr. and Mrs. F. to Number–," and "Auction–Model 1934," in F. Scott Fitzgerald, *The Crack-Up*, edited by Edmund Wilson (New York, 1945), pp. 41-62.

2. The references here are to *The Hamlet, The Town,* and *The Mansion,* and to *Sanctuary*, with its sequel, *Requiem for a Nun.*

3. See Chapter 4, I, where I discuss this matter.

4. The metaphor is Wescott's own. Later, for example, between 1928 and 1940, when he was unable to complete any of the many novels he began, he referred to them as his "abortions." Kahn p. 517.

5. I have taken this quotation out of context and applied it to Alwyn Tower. In the novel, the passage describes Alwyn's mother's relation to God; however, I think it can be applied to Alywn Tower without violence or distortion.

Chapter Four

1. Beach, *Twentieth Century Novel*, p. 479.

2. Sherman Paul, "Paul Rosenfeld," *Port of New York* (Urbana, Illinois; 1961), pp. xli ff.

3. Though Sullivan died in 1924, what Sherman Paul demonstrates in the book is that many of the ideas discussed here had been part of the American intellectual atmosphere from 1900 on and that many of them belong to what Mr. Paul calls the "Emersonian Tradition" and thus may be traced even farther back than this.

4. Paul, *Port of New York*, p. xlii.

5. *Ibid.*, p. xliii.

6. Beach, *Twentieth Century Novel*, p. 479.

7. For additional commentary on the love theme and the stories, all of it excellent, see Kahn, p. 145ff.; C. E. Schorer, *College English*, XVIII, 322, 325.

8. The three books referred to here are C. S. Lewis, *The Allegory of Love*, Denis de Rougemont, *Love in the Western World*, and Leslie Fiedler, *Love and Death in the American Novel.*

9. I have altered the syntax slightly here by replacing "there would be" with "is," but I do not think I have really altered the sense of the passage.

10. According to some of his friends, Wescott is an excellent performer, a man who puts on a good show. His role-acting can certainly be seen in the "Good-Bye Wisconsin" essay; and later, in *The Babe's Bed* and *The Pilgrim Hawk*, one can see Wescott's powerful fictional reaction against his performing self.

11. Wescott actually tried to write these two works: he repeatedly aborted the first, which was the utopian novel, "The Dream of Mrs. Cleveland," and finally published what he could salvage of it as "Hurt Feelings." The second one is *A Calendar of Saints for Unbelievers.*

12. Kahn, p. 185.

Chapter Five

1. Kahn, p. 191.

2. *Ibid.,* p. 306.

3. Letter from Glenway Wescott to the author, dated July 18, 1962.

4. A listing here would serve no useful purpose; for, if one takes the trouble to go through the relevant books, one finds that the references are passing ones and add little or nothing to one's understanding of Wescott.

5. *A Calendar of Saints for Unbelievers* was first published by Harrison of Paris in 1932; then by Harper & Brothers in 1933.

6. See, for example, all five of E. M. Forster's novels, but especially *A Room with a View,* where the concern with perception is actually incorporated into the title.

7. This quotation could be applied to all of the Towers in *The Grandmothers,* including Alwyn, and is an excellent description of what might be called "Tower's disease."

8. This quotation could serve as a description of what Wescott was trying to do in *Apartment in Athens.*

9. *The Pilgrim Hawk,* like *The Babe's Bed,* is centrally concerned with this problem: both are fictions about the dangers inherent in fiction-making. Thirty years later, in *Images of Truth,* Wescott was to make these same points again, at great length.

10. *The Pilgrim Hawk* is a good example of the first kind of truth listed below; and *Apartment in Athens* is a good example of the second. A similar listing appears in *Images of Truth,* p. 17.

11. It can be seen in the *New Republic* reviews discussed in Chapter I and, most notably, in the essay "Good-Bye Wisconsin." See also footnote 10 for Chapter 4.

Chapter Six

1. Kahn, pp. 509-10.

2. The essay-review on Katherine Anne Porter, "Praise," will be taken up later since it was incorporated into *Images of Truth* along with other pieces Wescott has written about her over the years.

3. Sy Kahn points out that "Though Wescott has been generous with information concerning his early work he has been understandably reticent to speak about his 'abortions' as he calls them." Kahn, p. 517.

4. "Three Men of the Twenties," p. 9. See the Bibliography, Primary Sources, Unpublished Material, for a description of this document.

5. Kahn, p. 362. According to my own list, Wescott has abandoned at least seven books, but of course it is impossible to know how much of each he wrote before giving it up.

Chapter Seven

1. This passage states one of the major themes of *The Pilgrim Hawk* and is one of the keys to the bird symbolism in all of Wescott's work.

2. The analysis of *The Pilgrim Hawk* which follows is peculiar in the sense that it is quite short and in no way attempts an exhaustive reading of the work. The novel is such that only a very close interpretation which followed the work page by page could really do it justice, and such an analysis is impossible in a brief study like this one. What I have aimed at here is an analysis of the novel in context, and to this end I have concentrated almost entirely upon Alwyn Tower as a figure for Wescott the novelist and followed his movements through the work. As a consequence, I have hardly discussed the way in which the subtitle— *A Love Story*—applies, nor have I said much about the Cullens and the ways in which their relationship functions in the novel as one of the realities. I plan to write of *The Pilgrim Hawk* at greater length in another book, and perhaps there I can analyze this remarkable novel as I think it ought to be done.

3. *The Pilgrim Hawk* is Westcott's *Great Gatsby*, only it took him sixteen instead of four years to produce it; and no *Tender is the Night* has come after to continue the development.

4. The best analysis of *The Pilgrim Hawk* I know of is Morton Dauwe Zabel's in *Craft and Character in Modern Fiction* (New York, 1957), pp. 304-8. Though it is extremely brief, it is also an excellent essay on Wescott as an American novelist.

5. For Wescott's idea of the ideal novel, see the discussion of *Images of Truth*, Chapter 6.

Chapter Eight

1. See *Images of Truth*, pp. 309-11.

2. Much of the material in *Images of Truth* on Katherine Anne Porter was originally written as book reviews, but Wescott almost always broke the form and ended up writing essay-reviews which he adjusted to his own particular inclinations. As a footnote to this footnote, I must add that writers are always making bad prophets out of critics. Between October, 1963, and July, 1964, Wescott published three front-page reviews in *Book Week* and there is no reason to suppose that he won't go on in this way.

Notes and References

3. See *Images of Truth*, pp. 309-10.

4. According to Kenneth Burke, this transcript is not always accurate because various remarks are mistakenly attributed. However, the two passages I quoted earlier could not have been said by anyone but Wescott.

5. I mention all of this to indicate that, though I had only seen Wescott publicly on Camera Three when I wrote this, it was possible to study his manner in the printed texts and, by combining this with my own limited observation, that of others who know him, and published observations on Wescott as a talker, to draw conclusions about the nature and significance of his public performances. I have since met Wescott, and let my conclusions stand.

6. "Autobiographical Note," *Images of Truth*.

7. The titles of these three essays are as follows: "I Love New York," (1943) "A Day in the Country," (1947) and "The Best of All Possible Worlds" (1959). Like all of Wescott's best work, they are almost impossible to analyze adequately except very closely, for they are almost all texture and detail and no summary of the main points could possibly give one any sense of what they are or what they are about.

Chapter Nine

1. It would certainly be unfair, however, not to point out that, as in all of his critical essays, Wescott does say many perceptive things about the authors and works which he discusses and that he does defend most passionately an approach to literature and life which transcends the individual self. One can see Wescott at his idiosyncratic best as a critic in "The Moral of F. Scott Fitzgerald."

2. Quoting Proust, Wescott suggests that this objectivity would be like "viewing the universe with the eyes of a hundred people" (*Images of Truth*, p. 25). Such objectivity is, of course, impossible; even in the work of Katherine Anne Porter, who tried so hard to achieve it, the self breaks through and one realizes, finally, that one is viewing the universe through the eyes of a single self.

3. See "Fiction Writing in a Time of Troubles," *Images of Truth*, pp. 3-24. The key passage is on p. 8.

Chapter Ten

1. I consider the following essays first-rate criticism: "Praise," *Southern Review*, V (1939), 161-73, which is the original essay-review of Katherine Anne Porter's *Pale Horse, Pale Rider;* "The Moral of F. Scott Fitzgerald"; and "Isak Dinesen, The Story Teller," which is Chapter 6 of *Images of Truth*.

2. See Patrick F. Quinn, "The Case History of Glenway Wescott," *Frontier and Midland*, XIX (1938-1939), 11-16.

3. See Granville Hicks, *The Great Tradition* (New York, 1933), pp. 277-83.

4. This interpretation can be found in Mr. Quinn's essay on pages 11-12, in the two essays discussed at length in the following paragraphs, and in Dayton Kohler's "Glenway Wescott: Legend-Maker," *Bookman*, LXXIII (1931), 142-45. The idea is also obsessive with Wescott: it is the Tower destiny which Alwyn attempts to escape in *The Grandmothers* but to which, by *The Pilgrim Hawk*, he seems to have succumbed.

5. I would like to point out here that not enough has been written on Wescott to enable one to document this paragraph in the way that one could a comparable paragraph on F. Scott Fitzgerald. However, Edwin Fussell's extraordinary essay on Fitzgerald's life and work as a lesson in American cultural history, which is included in Frederick Hoffman's *The Great Gatsby: A Study,* (New York, 1962), is an example of the kind of analysis which could be made of Wescott's life and works.

6. Marjorie Brace, "Thematic Problems of the American Novelist," *Accent*, VI (1945), 44-53.

7. C. E. Schorer, "The Maturing of Glenway Wescott," *College English*, XVIII (1957), 320-26.

8. Miss Brace also points out that, since the novel has failed, it is being "superceded by an experimental mixture of autobiography, philosophy and prose-poem" (*Accent*, VI, 44). This is a reasonably accurate description of what one finds in *Images of Truth* and in all of Wescott's lyric essays.

Selected Bibliography

Selected Bibliography

PRIMARY SOURCES

1. *Books*

The Bitterns, A Book of Twelve Poems. Evanston, Illinois: Monroe Wheeler, 1920.

The Apple of the Eye. New York: The Dial Press, 1924.

Natives of Rock: XX Poems: 1921-1922. Decorations by Pamela Bianco. New York: Francesco Bianco, 1925.

The Grandmothers, A Family Portrait. New York: Harper & Brothers, 1927; Harper's Modern Classics Edition, 1950; Atheneum Paperback Edition, 1962.

Good-Bye Wisconsin. New York: Harper & Brothers, 1928; Signet Edition, 1964.

The Babe's Bed. Paris: Harrison of Paris, 1930.

Fear and Trembling. New York: Harper & Brothers, 1932.

A Calendar of Saints for Unbelievers. Paris: Harrison of Paris, 1932; New York: Harper & Brothers, 1933.

The Pilgrim Hawk, A Love Story. New York: Harper & Brothers, 1940. Included in *Great American Short Novels*, edited by William Phillips, New York: Dial Press, 1946; and in *Six Great Modern Short Novels*, New York: Dell First Edition, 1954.

Apartment in Athens, New York: Harper & Brothers, 1945.

Twelve Fables of Aesop. Newly narrated by Glenway Wescott. Linoleum Blocks by Antonio Frasconi. New York: The Museum of Modern Art, 1954; Paperback Edition, n.d. [1964].

Images of Truth: Remembrances and Criticism. New York: Harper & Row, 1962; Harper Colophon Edition, 1964.

2. *Essays, Poems, Reviews, and Stories*

"Classics in English" [Review of *Sappho* by H. T. Wharton, *The Golden Treasury of the Greeks*, by A. L. Lothian, *Medallions in Clay* by R. Aldington, and *The Poets' Translation Series: Second Set*], *Poetry*, XVIII (1921), 284-88.

"Still Hunt" [Six Poems], *Poetry*, XVIII (1921), 303-7.

"New Fire" [Review of *A Canopic Jar* by Leonora Speyer], *Poetry*, XIX (1921), 47-51.

"Alexander Blok" [Review of *The Twelve* by Alexander Blok], *Poetry*, XIX (1921), 149-51.

"A Sonneteer" [Review of *Poems* by Stewart Mitchell], *Poetry*, XX (1922), 49-51.

"The Crocodile's Tears" [Review of *Neighbors Henceforth* by Owen Wister], *New Republic*, XXXIII (1923), 206, 208.

"The Two-Dollar Novel" [Omnibus Review of fiction], *New Republic,* XXXV (1923), 158-59.

"The Gift Horse" [Review of *Futility* by William Gerhardi], *New Republic,* XXXV (1923), 214.

"Sense and Sensibility" [Review of *One Hundred Best Books* and *Samphire* by John Cowper Powys], *New Republic,* XXXVI (1923), 26-27.

"Men Like Birds" [Poem], *Contact,* No. 5 (June, 1923).

"Named Flamingo" [Poem], *The Dial,* LXXV (1923), 264.

"The First Book of Mary Butts" [Review of *Speed the Plough and Other Stories* by Mary Butts], *The Dial,* LXXV (1923), 282-84.

"Impure Splendor" [Review of *Escapade* by Evelyn Scott], *Broom,* V (1923), 233-35.

"Old Style of Garden" [Poem], *The Little Review,* Spring, 1924.

"Concerning Miss Moore's Observations" [Review of *Observations* by Marianne Moore], *The Dial,* LXXVIII (1925), 1-4.

"A Historian of Conquests" [Review of *Hernando De Soto* by R. B. Cunningham Graham], *The Dial,* LXXVIII (1925), 417-19.

"Mr. Osbert Sitwell's Fiction" [Review of *Triple Fugue* by Osbert Sitwell], *The Dial,* LXXVIII (1925), 506-7.

"The Quarter's Books" [Essay-Review], *The Transatlantic Review,* II (1925), 446-48.

"A Monument" [Review of *The Spanish Farm* by R. H. Mottram], *The Dial,* LXXIX (1925), 246-47.

"A Courtly Poet" [Review of *A Draft of Sixteen Cantos* by Ezra Pound], *The Dial,* LXXIX (1925), 501-3.

"Miss Roberts' First Novel" [Review of *The Time of Man* by E. M. Roberts], *The Dial,* LXXXIII (1927), 73-75.

"Elizabeth Madox Roberts: A Personal Note" [Essay], *The Bookman,* LXXI (1930), 12-15.

"Hurt Feelings" [Story], *The North American Review,* CCXXXIV (1932), 223-40.

"A Sentimental Contribution" [Essay on Henry James], *Hound and Horn,* VII (1933-1934), 523-34.

"Poor Grueze" [Art Criticism], *Wadsworth Atheneum,* XIII (1935), 2-8.

"The Rescuer" [Story], *Life and Letters Today,* XV (Autumn, 1936), 150-56.

"The Sight of a Dead Body" [Story], *Signatures,* I (1936), 135-36.

"Biography and Impression," Leaflet for the Julien Levy Gallery Concerning the Painter Kristian Tonny, 23 February 1937–15 March 1937.

"A Commentary," Leaflet for the Julien Levy Gallery Announcing the Exhibition of the Murals of Jared French, 24 January 1939–7 February, 1939.

"The Summer Ending" [Poem], *Poetry,* LIV (1939), 306-7.

"The Dream of Audubon, Libretto of a Ballet in Three Scenes," *The Best One-Act Plays of 1940.* Ed. by Margaret Mayorga. New York: Dodd, Mead & Company, 1941, pp. 361-74.

"Personal and Otherwise" [Autobiographical Note], *Harper's Magazine,* CLXXXI (November, 1940), n.p.

"The Moral of F. Scott Fitzgerald" [Essay, originally published in 1941], *The Crack-Up*. Ed. by Edmund Wilson. New York: New Directions, 1945, pp. 323-37.

"Mr. Auerbach in Paris" [Story], *Harper's Magazine*, CLXXXIV (1941-42), 469-73.

"Personal and Otherwise" [Autobiographical Note], *Harper's Magazine*, CLXXXIV (April, 1942), n.p.

"The Frenchman Six Feet Three" [Story], *Harper's Magazine*, CLXXXV (1942), 131-40.

[Autobiographical Essay], *Twentieth Century Authors*. Ed. by S. J. Kunitz and Howard Haycraft. New York: The H. W. Wilson Company, 1942, pp. 1498-1500.

"Erich Maria Remarque," Leaflet for the Knoedler Galleries Announcing the Showing of the Remarque Collection of Paintings, 18 October 1943–18 November 1943.

"I Love New York" [Essay], *Harper's Bazaar*, LXXVII, Part 2 (December, 1943), 53, 55, 58, 104, 106, 108, 111.

"Stories by a Writer's Writer" [Review of *The Leaning Tower* by K. A. Porter], New York *Times Book Review*, 17 September 1944, p. 1.

"A Day in the Country" [Essay], *Tomorrow*, IX (July, 1947), 35-37.

"Love for a Traitor" [Review of *The Heat of the Day* by Elizabeth Bowen], *The Saturday Review*, XXXII (19 February 1949), 9-10.

"In Praise of Dr. Edith Sitwell," *Proceedings of the American Academy of Arts and Letters, and the National Institute of Arts and Letters*, Second Series, No. 1, 1951, pp. 49-52.

"Presentation to Marianne Moore of the Gold Medal for Poetry," *Proceedings of the American Academy of Arts and Letters, and the National Institute of Arts and Letters*, Second Series, No. 4, 1954, pp. 11-13.

[Autobiographical Essay], *Twentieth Century Authors*. Ed. by S. J. Kunitz and Howard Haycraft. New York: The H. W. Wilson Company, 1955, p. 1067.

"The Old and the New" [Opening remarks for an exhibit of paintings], *Proceedings of the American Academy of Arts and Letters, and the National Institute of Arts and Letters*, Second Series, No. 5, 1955, pp. 69-71.

"Introduction to a Reading by Robert Frost, 11 December 1955," *Proceedings of the American Academy of Arts and Letters, and the National Institute of Arts and Letters*, Second Series, No. 6, 1956, pp. 67-68.

[A Reading, with Louise Bogan, of their favorite poems by contemporary poets], *Proceedings of the American Academy of Arts and Letters, and the National Institute of Arts and Letters*, Second Series, No. 6, 1956, pp. 71-72.

"Presentation to Lincoln Kirstein of the Award for Distinguished Service to the Arts," *Proceedings of the American Academy of Arts and Letters, and the National Institute of Arts and Letters*, Second Series, No. 9, 1959, p. 266.

"The Best of All Possible Worlds" [Essay], *Proceedings of the American Academy of Arts and Letters, and the National Institute of Arts and Letters,* Second Series, No. 9, 1959, pp. 277-89.

"Presentation of Grants and Awards," *Proceedings of the American Academy of Arts and Letters, and the National Institute of Arts and Letters,* Second Series, No. 10, 1960, pp. 324-25.

"Presentation of Grants and Awards," *Proceedings of the American Academy of Arts and Letters, and the National Institute of Arts and Letters,* Second Series, No. 11, 1961, pp. 29-30.

"Statement [on censorship] Read at the Council Meeting February 3, 1959," *Proceedings of the American Academy of Arts and Letters, and the National Institute of Arts and Letters,* Second Series, No. 11, 1961, pp. 71-73.

"Not a Proper Englishman" [Review of *The Fifth Queen* by Ford Madox Ford], *Book Week,* 27 October 1963, pp. 1, 10.

"A Surpassing Sequel" [Review of *The Wapshot Scandal,* by John Cheever], *Book Week,* 5 January 1964, pp. 1, 9.

"All of Us on the Half-Shell" [Review of *The Oysters of Locmariaquer* by Eleanor Clark], *Book Week,* 12 July 1964, pp. 1, 14.

3. *Unpublished Material*

"The Best of All Possible Worlds." Expanded and revised typescript version of the essay originally published in the *Proceedings of the American Academy of Arts and Letters, and the National Institute of Arts and Letters,* Second Series, No. 9, 1959, pp. 277-89. Sent to the author by Glenway Wescott in 1962.

"Three Men of the Twenties." The three men are Gilbert Seldes, Kenneth Burke, and Glenway Wescott. The document is a transcript from tape of these three talking about the 1920's. The program was broadcast from the University of Wisconsin radio station in June, 1962. A copy was sent to the author by Glenway Wescott.

"Memories of the Twenties." Typescript version of the concluding section sent to the author by Glenway Wescott in 1962.

Letter to the author from Glenway Wescott dated July 18th, 1962.

"Camera Three." CBS television program on 23 September 1962 devoted to E. E. Cummings in which Glenway Wescott was one of the participants.

SECONDARY SOURCES

BEACH, JOSEPH WARREN. *The Twentieth Century Novel: Studies in Technique.* New York: D. Appleton-Century Company, 1932. Though there are only two pages (478-79) of specific comment on Wescott, both are excellent. Mr. Beach characterizes Wescott's technique, places him among his contemporaries, relates his work to other developments in the modern novel, and locates one of Wescott's central weaknesses as a novelist.

Selected Bibliography

BRACE, MARJORIE. "Thematic Problems of the American Novelist," *Accent*, VI (1945), 44-53. This is one of the most suggestive of all the essays on Wescott's fiction. See my detailed commentary in Chapter 10.

BURKE, KENNETH. "Delight and Tears," *The Dial*, LXXVII (1924), 513-15. This excellent review of *The Apple of the Eye* is particularly valuable for Mr. Burke's comments on it as a lyric novel.

————. "A Decade of American Fiction," *Bookman*, LXIX (1929), 561-67. Only page 566 is devoted to *Good-Bye Wisconsin* but everything said there is very good. Mr. Burke says again, correctly, that Wescott's talent is essentially lyric, and suggests some of the ways in which the stories may be read as symbolic autobiography. Like some other critics—C. E. Schorer, for example—he says there is a faint odor of "corruption" about Wescott's work. Mr. Burke has also analyzed *The Grandmothers* as symbolic autobiography in his *Philosophy of Literary Form*.

————. "The Poet and the Passwords," *New Republic*, LXXI (1932), 310-13. In this essay-review of *Fear and Trembling*, Mr. Burke accurately locates many of the things which are wrong with the book.

COWLEY, MALCOLM. *Exile's Return*. New York: The Viking Press, 1951. This is probably the best book we have on the expatriate movement and one of the best on the 1920's. It is very helpful toward understanding Wescott's relation to his times and specifically his involvement in the expatriate movement.

HATCHER, HARLAN. *Creating the Modern American Novel*. New York: Farrar & Rinehart, 1935. Mr. Hatcher has written an unusually good brief comment on Wescott's development through *Fear and Trembling*.

HICKS, GRANVILLE. *The Great Tradition, An Interpretation of American Literature since the Civil War*. New York: The Macmillan Company, 1933. Wescott is treated in a section called "Regionalism" in the last chapter of this book, which is entitled "Trumpet Call" and deals with a variety of solutions, mostly unsatisfactory according to Mr. Hicks, to the fundamental modern problems. Wescott's regional works are used to show why regionalism is a failure because it stresses sectional differences rather than national unity. Mr. Hicks treats Wescott's expatriation as a flight from reality and an abdication of responsibility.

HOFFMAN, FREDERICK J. *The Twenties*. New York: The Viking Press, 1951. This is a very useful book for understanding the literary situation in the twenties and Wescott's relation to it.

————, CHARLES ALLEN, and CAROLYN F. ULRICH. *The Little Magazine*. Princeton University Press, 1951. This book is both a fascinating chapter in the literary history of the 1920's and 1930's and an indispensable bibliographical tool.

KAHN, SY MYRON. *Glenway Wescott: A Critical and Biographical Study*, Ann Arbor: University Microfilms, 1957, Publication number 20,631. Anyone who writes on Wescott must be profoundly indebted to Mr. Kahn: most of the facts about Wescott's life which one has to work with are to be found in his dissertation; he contributes extensively to one's understanding of many of the works; the manuscript versions of portions of *The Grandmothers* enable one to study Wescott at work; and the Wescott–Harper & Brothers correspondence enables one to follow Wescott's development from the inside.

————. "Glenway Wescott: A Bibliography," *Bulletin of Bibliography*, XXII (1956-1959), 156-60. As Mr. Kahn says, "Part One of this bibliography chronologically presents Mr. Wescott's work and is intended to be exhaustive." Though I have never come across anything before 1954—Kahn's cut-off date—which is not in Kahn's bibliography, Wescott says that a "few" items are missing. The bibliography gives the publishing history, including translations. "Part Two is a selective bibliography of critical writings about Wescott" and "includes all major articles, books with substantial sections on Wescott, and reviews of outstanding quality." Like his dissertation, Mr. Kahn's bibliography is indispensable to anyone wishing to study Wescott.

KOHLER, DAYTON. "Glenway Wescott: Legend Maker," *Bookman*, LXXIII (1931), 142-45. Mr. Dayton's essay-review of *The Babe's Bed* is one of the best commentaries and appreciations of Wescott's regional works; he is also very good on Wescott's retrospective narrative method.

MILLET, FRED. "Introduction" *The Grandmothers*. Harper's Modern Classics Edition. New York: Harper & Brothers, 1950. Mr. Millet has provided a useful, brief summary of and comment on Wescott's life and career as well as a good commentary on *The Grandmothers*, especially on the unique form of the novel.

PAUL, SHERMAN. "Paul Rosenfeld," *Port of New York*. Urbana: University of Illinois Press, 1961. Though the whole of the fine introductory essay contributes to one's understanding of the period, it is Section II which is especially relevant to Wescott, for there Mr. Paul defines and discusses the myth of America which is so central to *The Grandmothers*, and characterizes the period out of which the novel came.

QUINN, PATRICK F. "The Case History of Glenway Wescott," *Frontier and Midland*, XIX (1938-1939), 11-16. Mr. Quinn treats Wescott as a representative expatriate and uses him as a case history to show why the expatriates should have stayed home. His secondary point is that Wescott should have stuck to writing short stories. I think Mr. Quinn wrong on both counts, but he says some interesting things about Wescott.

ROSENFELD, PAUL. *Port of New York*. Urbana: University of Illinois Press, 1961. Originally published in 1924, this collection of essays by Paul Rosenfeld is one of the best introductions to the period. To read Rosenfeld's essay on Van Wyck Brooks concurrently with *The Grandmothers* is a good way to understand and appreciate that novel.

SCHORER, C. E., "The Maturing of Glenway Wescott," *College English*, XVIII (1957), 320-26. Mr. Schorer's is the best single essay on Wescott. See my detailed commentary in Chapter 10.

Selected Bibliography

SUCKOW, RUTH. "Middle Western Literature," *The English Journal,* XXI (1932), 175-82. In her excellent discussion of Midwestern regional literature, what it is, and how it takes on universal significance, Miss Suckow ranks *The Grandmothers* among the major Midwestern works and comments very perceptively upon its tone and style.

ZABEL, MORTON DAUWE. "The Whisper of the Devil," *Craft and Character in Modern Fiction.* New York: The Viking Press, 1957. Originally written as a review of *The Pilgrim Hawk,* this is the best single commentary on *The Pilgrim Hawk* and a most penetrating analysis of Wescott's techniques as a fiction writer.

Index

Thurber, James, 127
Tolstoy, Leo, 82
Transatlantic Review, The, 30, 33, 36, 70
Twelve Fables of Aesop, 122, 126-28
Twenties, The, 24, 36-38, 57-58, 71, 141, 150

Vogue Magazine, 142

Welty, Eudora, 105
Wescott, Glenway, as poet, 23-24, 25-30, 143, 152, 157; development of, 23-25, 31-32, 33, 39-40, 45, 46-47, 61-63, 71-74, 75-79, 88-90, 91-93, 101-3, 104-5, 107-8, 115, 119-21, 122-23, 129-30, 131-32, 138-40, 141-53 *passim;* as reviewer, 24, 30-36, 122, 123, 143, 160; as novelist, 24, 59-61, 141-53 *passim;* as regional writer, 24-25, 31, 40-45, 46-56, 57-74 *passim*, 89-90, 92, 95, 141, 142, 144, 150; and expatriation, 25, 36-38, 46-56 *passim*, 89-90, 91, 113, 141, 144, 149, 150; his idea of the novel, 34-36, 36-38, 39-40, 84-85, 92-93, 100-1, 120, 133-40 *passim;* relation of works to life, 40-41, 44, 54, 108, 158; main themes of, 60; as short story writer, 61-68; as cultural critic, 79-85, 143, 150; as hagiographer, 85-90, 143; as literary critic, 99-102, 131-40, 152, 161; as public lecturer, 123-24, 143, 161; reputation of, 141-43; as essayist, *see* Lyric essay; as ballet librettist, 104-7, 143; as art critic, 143; as worker for the arts, 24, 122, 123, 124-26, 143; as an American writer, 144-53 *passim*, 162; abandoned works of, 91-98 *passim*, 102-3, 160
Wescott, Lloyd, 91
Wheeler, Monroe, 23, 75, 91, 126
White, E. B., 83, 102, 128
Wilder, Thornton, 137, 157
Williams, William Carlos, 37
Wilson, Edmund, 89, 143
Winters, Yvor, 23, 37, 157
Wister, Owen, 32
World War II, 107, 114-21

Yeats, William Butler, 81